HOW TO WRITE A WINNING RESUME

HOW TO WRITE A WINNING RESUME

Deborah P. Bloch, Ph.D.

Fourth Edition

VGM Career Horizons
NTC/Contemporary Publishing Group

Library of Congress Cataloging-in-Publication Data

Bloch, Deborah Perlmutter.
    How to write a winning resume / Deborah P. Bloch. — 4th ed.
       p.   cm.
    ISBN 0-8442-6692-2
    1. Résumés (Employment)   I. Title.
HF5383.B53   1998
650′ 14—dc21   98-20710
                                       CIP

Acknowledgments

My thanks go to the many friends and colleagues who participated in the interviews for this book and shared many examples of resumes.
    A very special thank you must be said to my husband, Martin Bloch, who provided essential support ranging from alphabetizing to zucchini slicing.

    Author's note: the names of all individuals and companies, as well as the addresses and phone numbers used in examples, sample resumes, and cover letters in this book are fictional.

Published by VGM Career Books
A division of NTC/Contemporary Publishing Group, Inc.
4255 West Touhy Avenue, Lincolnwood (Chicago), Illinois 60712-1975 U.S.A.
Printed in the United States of America
International Standard Book Number: 0-8442-6692-2
0 0 01 02 03 04 05 VH 19 19 18 17 16 15 14 13 12 11 10 9 8 7 6 5 4 3 2

Contents

About the Author

Deborah P. Bloch, Ph.D., is the author of four books designed to help people find the jobs that are right for them. These books, all in the VGM Career Horizons series, have sold more than 150,000 copies. Dr. Bloch is also the author of books for individuals, counselors, and educators on the spiritual aspects of work, factors that enhance the sense of wholeness in career.

Dr. Bloch has focused her work on the career development of individuals and the organizational structures that promote a healthy work environment. She is associate professor of Organization and Leadership at the University of San Francisco. Previously, she was at Baruch College of the City University of New York. In addition to her university work, Dr. Bloch has worked as a consultant in the United States and abroad. She has served as president of both the National Career Development Association and the Association of Computer-Based Systems for Career Information. She is a member of the editorial board of the *Career Planning and Adult Development Journal*. Dr. Bloch has received the Distinguished Service Award of the Association of Computer-Based Systems for Career Information, the Resource Award of the Career Planning and Adult Development Network, and the Merit Award of the National Career Development Association.

Her work includes many published, professional articles and numerous workshops for counselors and others who help people with their career decisions and job searches.

Other books by Dr. Bloch include:

Published by VGM Career Horizons:

- *How to Have a Winning Job Interview* (3rd Edition);

- *How to Make the Right Career Moves* (suggestions for people in mid-career); and

- *How to Get a Good Job and Keep It* (help for high school students and others just starting out).

Published by Davies-Black Publishing:

- *SoulWork: Finding the Work You Love; Loving the Work You Have* (with Dr. Lee J. Richmond); and

- *Connections Between Spirit and Work in Career Development: New Approaches and Practical Perspectives* (a set of original readings edited by Deborah P. Bloch and Lee J. Richmond).

Deborah P. Bloch, Ph.D. and Lee J. Richmond, Ph.D. are trainers, consultants, and researchers offering services to corporations and other organizations interested in connecting spirit and work for organizational growth through individual well-being. You can learn more about the services and products of their firm, SBR Consults, in any of the following ways:

Visit their Web site at *http://www.careerconsults.com*

Send them e-mail at *sbr@careerconsults.com*

Write to them at SBR Career Consults, 1032 Irving Street, #980, San Francisco, CA 94122-2200

Call them—415-566-5395 (West Coast) or 410-250-5391 (East Coast)

How to use this book: Read this before you begin!

Your resume is your entry pass to a successful job search. Your resume brings your skills, talents, and experiences before your potential employers in a written form designed to engage their interest. But we know that with computers, written forms and information resources are changing. The biggest challenge you face right now is how to use the right technology to maximize the effectiveness of your resume.

The most important thing to remember is that while technology has changed how we present ideas, human nature has not changed. Your prospective employer is still looking for the best person to do the job. He or she still has a mental image of the mix of education, skills, talents, experiences that have shaped the ideal candidate. It is still the job of the resume writer, your job, to present what you know and what you have done to the best possible advantage. It is still your job to sort through all that you know and all that you have done so that your resume matches the mental image of the ideal held by the employer. It is your job to write a winning resume.

This is the fourth edition of *How to Write a Winning Resume*. Tens of thousands of readers have used the strategies presented in the previous editions to help them achieve success in their job search. This edition continues to include those basic strategies because they still work! But this edition has something entirely new. It helps you utilize the power of the computer and the even greater power of the Internet to sharpen the focus of your resume, to identify new places to send your resume, and to format your resume so that it can be read by both machines and humans.

All technologies you will use to present your skills, talents, and experiences end as written words that are seen by human eyes. But sometimes your resume will be read first by the human eye, with information only to be stored later in a computer, and other times your resume will first be screened by a computer and reach human eyes only if it passes that first screening. In *How to Write a Winning Resume*, you will learn the formatting techniques for e-mailed, Internet-submitted, scannable, and printed resumes. Please remember that print is still a technology that is in use! In fact, people I interviewed for this edition of the book still found their organizations required ordinary printed resumes, although these might be faxed instead of mailed. Even in many of the most high-tech companies, all screening of applicants' resumes was done by managers who read them, not by machines that scanned them.

However, I know of other companies that are using machine-scanning to sort resumes. They can do this by reading the printed resume into a computer with an optical scanning reader. They can then set up a program or simply use the "find" command of the edit section of their word processor to look for key words pertinent to any particular job. There are also resume scanning services available over the Internet. You submit your resume using a computer-generated form. The employer submits a job request with key words. The computer looks for a match—and bingo! At least "bingo" is what you hope for.

In the vast world of occupations and jobs, most companies remain "lower" tech, that is, print oriented. However, computer capabilities are increasing so quickly that the balance of machine versus human screening may change sooner than expected. In the not-too-distant future, more and more employers may be using resume scanning services to choose among applicants. This fourth edition of *How to Write a Winning Resume* will help you format your resume for today and the foreseeable future.

However, there is more to using computer technology than formatting your resume for human versus machine readability—or human *and* machine readability. Your computer, or the computer in your library, school, or office, can also help you choose the words that will stand out for the employer while remaining true to your own experience. Access to the Internet can help you identify more employers to receive your resume. It can also help you target your resume to the right person in an organization. And the Internet can give you more information about the organization that will receive your resume so that you can tailor your resume to the specific job requirements.

Each chapter contains specific hints on using the power of computing to enhance your resume. These sections are called "Techno-Tips." All the parts of all the chapters together will help you fulfill the purpose of the resume.

The Purpose of a Resume

The purpose of a resume is to get you considered for a job. It's not likely that anyone has ever gotten a job solely on the basis of her or his resume, but people often lose the chance to be considered in the first place because of poorly written or presented resumes. A winning resume speaks directly to the audience you want to reach.

Who is the audience for your resume? Are you looking for a first job, a new job, or a turnabout in career direction? The audience is each potential employer. There is also a new and growing way to work called contract employment. Contract workers provide specific services to businesses as they need them. If you want to take advantage of this end of the job market and independently contract out your services, your resume provides the written evidence of your experience and ability to the audience—the individual in the organization responsible for choosing the service.

If you have a variety of skills and services to offer, you can successfully run a "portfolio career." This means you are offering contracted services of varied types to equally varied businesses. Each edition of your resume can be geared to the service buyer whose needs you want to meet.

Even if you want to go into business on your own, a resume is probably needed as part of your business plan to convince prospective investors of your expertise and experience.

You know why you want to write a resume, but you may not be sure how to go about it. Questions of what to include and how to show yourself to best advantage are common. You may have heard terms like *functional* or *chronological* resume and wonder what they should mean to you. This book will help you understand what to include in your resume and how to present your information to the best advantage.

You may also have seen ads in newspapers and magazines for "experts" who can help you prepare a resume, and at this point, you may not really be sure that you should tackle this job on your own. Eliminate any self-doubt. *You are the best person to write your resume, because no one can know you, your skills, interests, and goals as well as you do.* A professional resume writer might be able to make the job seem easier, but you will find that you can do just as good a job on your own. And this book will help you make it even better.

This book provides a step-by-step guide to help you through the resume writing process. Your questions on what to include to put your best foot forward will be answered, and you will find by the time you finish the book that you understand the process very well.

Many of the suggestions included in this book are based on the advice of employers in industries such as banking, computers, insurance, advertising, accounting, education, health services, law, merchandising, and others. The people surveyed are responsible for hiring employees from entry-level jobs through middle management positions and experienced professionals to the highest-level executives. Although the employers came from a variety of fields, and they themselves ranged in age from 25 to over 65, their responses to the questions were remarkably similar. Therefore, when you see a quotation from the survey, you can know that one employer said it, but the thought represents the responses of many. The step-by-step approach used in this book is designed to help you produce the kind and quality of information that these professional managers have stated specifically that they want to see.

The purpose of the resume is to get you an interview! The resume must catch the attention of the reader so that it goes in the pile "to be considered," rather than the pile "to be discarded." A resume that makes the first pile and stays on top of it is a winning resume.

Steps to Your Goal

Your goal is to produce a winning resume—and there are essential steps in the logical sequence of right moves to reach that goal.

Step 1. Explore the details of your life for skills and accomplishments, names, dates, and places.

Step 2. Translate your skills and accomplishments into power terms and the language of the job you are seeking in the industry that interests you.

Step 3. Present the material in a way that holds the attention of the reader and reveals the very best about you.

Step 4. Write a cover letter that provides direction to the reader of your resume—your prospective employer or buyer of your services.

The chapters of this book will help you through these steps to reach your goal—a winning resume.

Chapter 1, Building blocks, includes a series of worksheets on which you will explore and develop your educational and occupational history. It includes a self-assessment questionnaire that will pinpoint the relationships between your abilities and a number of jobs.

Chapter 2, Show and tell—use nouns and verbs, shows you how to translate the building blocks into active, effective statements for your resume.

By the time you finish *Chapter 3, Assembly*, you will have a draft of your resume, and you will know how to prepare your resume for electronic media.

In *Chapter 4, Getting physical*, you will learn details of paper, layout, and typing. The mystique surrounding word processing, paper selection, and reproduction will be eliminated, probably saving you some money. *Chapter 4* concludes with specific directions for proofreading your resume.

You will see in *Chapter 5, Made to order*, how your resume can be tailored to reach employers in different fields, and how to customize your resume if you are in a special situation. This chapter will be of particular help if you are looking for your first job, if you are trying to change careers, or if you are returning to the workforce after having been unemployed for a while. You will see how to use the "Building blocks" in different ways.

Chapter 6, Cover letters and recordkeeping, is about how to write a cover letter, an essential part of each resume. It also includes suggestions for keeping track of resumes you've sent.

In all of the chapters, plenty of models and examples are given.

The last chapter, *Chapter 7, Beauty is in the eye of the beholder*, summarizes the advice given by the personnel officers who were interviewed for this book, and gives you their final checklist for do's and don'ts.

A list of *Related resources* at the end of the book provides ways and means of identifying recipients of your resume.

Finally, in Appendix C, you will find brief job descriptions. This will prove helpful to you in finding the right words and phrases for your resume and in thinking of the specific job titles of jobs you might want to seek.

HOW TO WRITE A WINNING RESUME

Building blocks

Build your winning resume from pages and pages of your work experience, career goals, and life details that are then carefully selected and rephrased.

The first step in preparing your resume is to gather the information that you have to work with. The use of computers to produce or transmit your resume has not altered the need for this step. The purpose of this chapter is to help you gather and write down a great deal of information about yourself that may be useful to you in preparing your resume. It is true that a brief, concise resume is the most effective, and you will want to be sure that the final form of your resume is not wordy, overdone, or long-winded. However, to begin with, you will need to take stock of all the experience, knowledge, and skills that you have to offer.

Consider Chapter 1 as your *information builder.* In each of the sections you will have a chance to jot down all the details you can think of. You will never use them all in the final version of your resume; you will *choose* the details that are most applicable to the job you want. But before

1

you can choose the best items to include, you will need to develop good, long lists of personal notes. Don't be afraid to write down a seemingly minor activity or accomplishment. If you did it, you learned something from it, and it may be useful. Put it down on paper or in a computer file where you can look at it, and consider it as you build your resume.

A winning resume is built up step-by-step, using the elements which employers want to see quickly, and easily, as soon as they look at the resume.

For the purposes of this book, we will call these elements *Blocks*—they are the *Building Blocks* of all resumes. These Building Blocks include all the kinds of information that employers need in order to consider you for a job: information about your education and training, work history, and the like.

The first step in preparing your resume is to gather information about yourself, and write it all down. Later, you will refine this information, boil it down, and rewrite it in the best wording and the best order for the job you want to win.

Too many times, job applicants make the mistake of trying to write a rough draft of the whole resume. They try to write *brief statements,* and never really look at all the experience they have had, and all the work they have done.

In this section you will explore and identify the key work experiences and accomplishments of your life. To do this, you will explore, through writing, all of the areas of your life that are related to work. The areas are as follows:

Block A: Education and training

Block B: Certificates and licenses

Block C: Work history

Block D: Related experience such as consulting, teaching, or training others

Block E: Professional organizations, association memberships, and unions; committee memberships and offices held

Block F: Hobbies, community activities, volunteer work, and leisure activities

Block G: Special abilities related to your work such as knowledge of a foreign language

Block H: Publications or presentations at meetings, conferences, or conventions

Block I: Skills assessment questionnaire

The section "Techno-Tips," toward the end of the chapter, explains how you can use the computer to help you record the information.

Before beginning work on this chapter, look over the list of Building Blocks. Remember that this book is written to help many people, each of whom has had a different set of experiences. If one of the Building Blocks has no meaning for you, do not try to force your life to fit the book: just skip that block! For example, if you are not active in community organizations, or if you have never made a speech or presentation, or published an article, ignore those pages and concentrate on the Building Blocks that can be used to show the experience that you have had. In the spaces given for your Personal Notes, you can jot down informally your own experiences.

Block A: Education and Training

> *Concentrate on abilities, accomplishments, and energy you showed in school or college if you are a beginning worker.*

Use this Building Block to identify your accomplishments in education. If you are looking for your first or second job, this section is very important in your resume because this is the area in which you can show the ability and energy you have through the activities you took part in, in school. If you have been out of school and working for a while, or are well advanced in your career, then you will probably just want to list any degrees you have earned, any special coursework which is of particular relevance to the job you are seeking, and any honors you have been awarded. If you have taken recent additional courses, those may be useful to include, as well.

Complete each of the sections below with attention to detail of names and dates. If you are uncertain of the dates or spelling of names, circle the item for research later. Then come back to fill in the missing information. In each section, begin with the most recent and work backward into your past.

School History

In this section, you will list the names of all the schools you have attended, from high school to the present time.

You may have only one school to list, or you may have several.

Keep in mind:

- All of your education is important to list.

- Start by listing your most recent schooling first.

- This list *is not the final form* for your resume: it is for your own use.

Two examples of possible lists are included below to give you an idea of the kinds of schools you may want to list.

EXAMPLE

Name of School: New York University, New York, New York
Major or Area of Concentration: Business Administration
Degree or Credits Earned: Bachelor's Degree
Dates: September 1995–June 1999

EXAMPLE

Name of School: Price Academy of Business, Baltimore, Maryland
Major or Area of Concentration: Bookkeeping, Records Management
Degree or Credits Earned: None
Dates: September 1997–January 1998

Name of School: Parker High School, Baltimore, Maryland
Major or Area of Concentration: Accounting
Degree or Credits Earned: Diploma
Dates: September 1993–June 1997

Personal Notes

In the space below, write in all the school, college, and training programs you have completed. Be sure to write down all the educational background you have.

Name of School: _____

Major or Area of Concentration: _____

Degree or Credits Earned: _____

Dates: _____

Name of School: _____

Major or Area of Concentration: _____

Degree or Credits Earned: _____

Dates: _____

Name of School: _____

Major or Area of Concentration: _____

Degree or Credits Earned: _____

Dates: _____

Evidence of Knowledge

In this section you will want to think carefully of all the special courses or course content that you have had that might be of interest to the employer. If you were applying for a job as a carpenter, and you had also taken school courses in cabinet making, you would want to mention that special area of knowledge because it would qualify you for a broader field of jobs.

EXAMPLE

Course of Particular Interest: Systems Analysis
Relevance to Job: Seeking job in health services field. Field is increasingly computerized.

Personal Notes

Course of Particular Interest: _____

_____

Relevance to Job: _____

_____

Course of Particular Interest: _____

_____

Relevance to Job: _____

_____

Course of Particular Interest: _____

_____

Relevance to Job: _____

_____

Course of Particular Interest: _____

_____

Relevance to Job: _____

_____

Evidence of Independent Study

Many people neglect to mention special projects they have taken part in, where training may have contributed something of value to their educations or they revealed their energy or special skills. An employer may find that "something extra" in just such information. In this section, write down all the projects you have taken part in, on your own.

EXAMPLE

Special Projects and Papers: Worked on year-long project to aid elderly with nutritional needs.
Relevance to Job: Job requires skill with people of varied backgrounds.

Personal Notes

Special Project or Paper: _____

_____

Relevance to Job: _____

_____

Special Project or Paper: _____

_____

Relevance to Job: _____

_____

Special Project or Paper: _____

_____

Relevance to Job: _____

_____

Special Project or Paper: _____

_____

Relevance to Job: _____

_____

Evidence of Energy and Leadership

If you belonged to student or other organizations, held offices, or led fund-raising drives, these activities demonstrate your ability to take an active role in group activities. Jot down all those activities, to see which ones may apply when you write your resume.

EXAMPLE

Organization or Activity: Campus Daily Newspaper
Accomplishments: Served as business manager for two years.

Personal Notes

Organization or Activity: _____

_____

Accomplishments: _____

_____

Organization or Activity: _____

_____

Accomplishments: _____

_____

Organization or Activity: _____

_____

Accomplishments: _____

_____

Organization or Activity: _____

_____

Accomplishments: _____

_____

Honors

List here any awards, memberships in honorary societies, or special honors you have achieved. These might be strictly academic, or for some special achievement in sports, service clubs, or other activities. Be sure to include the name of the organization honoring you and the date of the award.

EXAMPLE

Honor: Dean's List, University of Michigan, Academic Years 1995–96, 1996–97, 1997–98.

Personal Notes

Honor: _____

Awarding Organization: _____

Dates: _____

Honor: _____

Awarding Organization: _____

Dates: _____

Now that you have finished Block A, review your educational history and fill in any missing dates. Be sure that you check on the accuracy of any items you circled as uncertain. Ask friends, family members, or instructors to look over your notes to see if you have forgotten anything that might prove useful.

Block B: Certificates and Licenses

Use this section to record the data on any certificates or licenses required for the job you are seeking. If you have applied for a certificate, but have not yet received it, use the phrase, "application pending."

License requirements vary by state. If you have moved, or you are planning to move to a different state, check with the appropriate board or licensing agency in the state in which you are seeking work to be sure you know the requirements.

Be sure that all of the information listed is completely accurate. Locate copies of your licenses and certificates, check the dates and exact names of accrediting agencies.

EXAMPLE

Name of License: Teacher of English, Permanent
Licensing Agency: State of New Jersey, Department of Education
Date Issued: 1999

Personal Notes

Name of License: _____

Licensing Agency: _____

Date Issued: _____

Name of License: _____

Licensing Agency: _____

Date Issued: _____

Name of License: _____

Licensing Agency: _____

Date Issued: _____

Block C: Work History

> *Use your work history as the central focus of your resume.*

This section will provide the central focus of your resume. When your resume is finished, the whole thing will be only one or two pages long. However, in filling out this block, it is important that you be as complete as possible. It is only by examining your experiences in depth, that you can get to the core of your accomplishments, and present them in a way that shows how strong your qualifications are. As you work, be aware of the need for accuracy. However, don't let a long search for a record that will tell you whether you left a job in May or June of 1988 distract you from the flow of self-examination and writing. When you are missing some detail, just circle that item and come back to it later.

Complete these sections in reverse chronological order as you did the items in *Block A: Education and Training*. Begin with the most recent, and work backward.

EXAMPLE

Job Title: Partner in charge of audits   **Dates:** 1995 to 1999
Employer: Martin and Company, Accountants
Address: 432 Madison Avenue
City, State, Zip: New York, NY 10017
Major Duties: Conducted audits of the following types of clients: public, multinational, multiplant manufacturing corporation; publishing company; investment advisory service; public housing and health services agencies. Prepared annual reports from clients to shareholders. Prepared corporate tax returns.
Special Projects: Helped clients in their selection of hardware and software for their internal accounting and bookkeeping systems. Utilized spreadsheet software in budgeting for clients and firm.
Evidence of Leadership: Was partner responsible for hiring in the firm. Initiated project to acquire and utilize intranet.
Evidence of Special Skills: I was frequently consulted by clients on their purchase of PCs. I wrote Visual BASIC applications with MS Access database.
Company Accomplishments for Which I Was Responsible: Through increased automation, the company was able to serve 20 percent more clients without increased personnel or operating costs.

Personal Notes

Job 1

Job Title: _____ **Dates:** _____

Employer: _____

Address: _____

City, State, Zip: _____

Major Duties: _____

_____

_____

Special Projects: _____

_____

_____

Evidence of Leadership: _____

_____

Evidence of Special Skills: _____

_____

Company Accomplishments for Which I Was Responsible: _____

_____

_____

Job 2

Job Title: _____ **Dates:** _____

Employer: _____

Address: _____

City, State, Zip: _____

Major Duties: _____

_____

_____

Special Projects: _____

_____

_____

Evidence of Leadership: _____

_____

_____

Evidence of Special Skills: _____

_____

_____

Company Accomplishments for Which I Was Responsible: _____

_____

_____

Job 3

Job Title: _____ **Dates:** _____

Employer: _____

Address: _____

City, State, Zip: _____

Major Duties: _____

_____

_____

Special Projects: _____

_____

_____

Evidence of Leadership: _____

_____

_____

Evidence of Special Skills: _____

_____

_____

Company Accomplishments for Which I Was Responsible: _____

_____

_____

Job 4

Job Title: _____ **Dates:** _____

Employer: _____

Address: _____

City, State, Zip: _____

Major Duties: _____

_____

_____

Special Projects: _____

_____

_____

Evidence of Leadership: _____

_____

_____

Evidence of Special Skills: _____

_____

Company Accomplishments for Which I Was Responsible: _____

_____

_____

Block D: Related Experience

In this section, you will review any experiences you have had, such as teaching or consulting, that are related to your work. Record any work you have done, whether paid work or volunteer, in which you helped others using skills or knowledge that are very similar to the skills and knowledge you use in your regular full-time employment.

Of course, if your regular full-time employment is teaching or consulting, then you would use the previous block, Block C: Work History, to record your experience. If you have done volunteer or community work that you feel is less directly related to your primary job, but which illustrates other skills, you may want to record that in Block F: Volunteer and Leisure Activities.

EXAMPLE

Job Title: Security Guard
Organization or Group Served: Morgan Township Baseball League
Dates: 1997–1999
Activities and Accomplishments: Trained parents of team members in handling parking lot and stadium security for summer season of games.

Personal Notes

Related Experience 1

Job Title: _____

Organization or Group Served: _____

Dates: _____

Activities and Accomplishments: _____

_____

Related Experience 2

Job Title: _____

Organization or Group Served: _____

Dates: _____

Activities and Accomplishments: _____

_____

Related Experience 3

Job Title: _____

Organization or Group Served: _____

Dates: _____

Activities and Accomplishments: _____

_____

Related Experience 4

Job Title: _____

Organization or Group Served: _____

Dates: _____

Activities and Accomplishments: _____

_____

Block E: Professional Associations

Use this section to record your activities in professional associations, unions, and other similar organizations. Be accurate in your dates. Review your areas of interest and involvement as a reminder of organizations you may want to list. If you have not been involved in professional associations, simply leave this section blank, and if you took part in special activities, or held any offices, be sure to jot those down, too.

EXAMPLE

Name of Organization: Nevada State Society of Cosmetologists
Activities or Offices Held, with Dates: President, 1998–1999; Chairperson of Membership Committee, 1997–1998

Personal Notes

Name of Organization: _____

Activities or Offices Held, with Dates: _____

_____

Name of Organization: _____

Activities or Offices Held, with Dates: _____

_____

Name of Organization: _____

Activities or Offices Held, with Dates: _____

_____

Name of Organization: _____

Activities or Offices Held, with Dates: _____

_____

Block F: Volunteer and Leisure Activities

> *Demonstrate your skills and energies through volunteer work.*

Use this section to review and record any important activities that you have pursued outside of work. These activities should not only be the ones that bring you pleasure, but those in that you have demonstrated your skills or your energies. This is another area that helps you to look at your accomplishments and put them into words.

You may have helped your religious group raise money for a special project. In that case, you have developed skills in fund-raising and managing a fund-raising team. Working for a political party in door-to-door voter campaigns or managing bake sales or rummage sales are all volunteer activities that demonstrate skill and energy.

If you are looking for your first job, or if you are a homemaker ready to enter or reenter the paid workforce, this block is a very important one for you.

EXAMPLE

Activity: Community center wall hanging project
Evidence of Skill: I organized over 200 people in the community to produce wall hangings for the community center. I solicited materials from local merchants who donated them free of charge.
Areas of Accomplishment: The community center had wall hangings. I was able to organize many people. I was able to sell an idea.

Personal Notes

Leisure Activity 1

Activity: _____

Evidence of Skill: _____

_____

_____

Areas of Accomplishment: _____

_____

_____

Leisure Activity 2

Activity: _____

Evidence of Skill: _____

_____

_____

Areas of Accomplishment: _____

_____

_____

Leisure Activity 3

Activity: _____

Evidence of Skill: _____

_____

_____

Areas of Accomplishment: _____

_____

_____

Leisure Activity 4

Activity: _____

Evidence of Skill: _____

_____

_____

Areas of Accomplishment: _____

_____

_____

Block G: Special Work-Related Abilities

In this section you can record any special abilities that you have. Think particularly of how these abilities are related to the job you are seeking.

Examples of abilities you might want to note in this section include: fluency in one or more foreign languages, familiarity with particular brands of computer hardware or software, security clearances, the ability to travel or to relocate.

EXAMPLE

Ability: Able to operate on both Windows and Macintosh platforms.

Personal Notes

Ability: _____

_____

Ability: _____

_____

Ability: _____

_____

Block H: Publications and Presentations

Use this section to record any articles you have written, professional papers you have had published, or any presentations you have made. In doing this, remember that your paper did not have to be published by a major publisher. It may have been published by your school or your company in its own magazine. Similarly, your presentation may have been before a school or local group, not before a large national crowd. All of these should be included.

In recording papers and presentations, italicize or underline the title of the publication. Use quotation marks around the title of an article or a presentation.

EXAMPLE OF AN ARTICLE

Title: "Employees Celebrate Bonus Year"
Journal or Organization: *Harcourt Paint and Glass Company Magazine*
Place: Denver, Colorado
Date: September 1998.

EXAMPLE OF A PRESENTATION

Title: "Using the Internet in Your Job Search"
Journal or Organization: United Career Counselors
Place: New York, New York
Date: November 1998

Personal Notes

Title: _____

Journal or Organization: _____

Place: _____

Date: _____

Title: _____

Journal or Organization: _____

Place: _____

Date: _____

Title: _____

Journal or Organization: _____

Place: _____

Date: _____

Title: _____

Journal or Organization: _____

Place: _____

Date: _____

Title: _____

Journal or Organization: _____

Place: _____

Date: _____

Title: _____

Journal or Organization: _____

Place: _____

Date _____

Block I: Skills Assessment

> *See how your strengths relate to jobs that interest you.*

In previous blocks, you looked at your personal history—in education, work, and other activities—to come up with a list of skills and accomplishments that will form the central core of your resume. This block will help you examine your abilities more directly, in relationship to the jobs you want to apply for.

The Skills Assessment Questionnaire that follows consists of 16 items. Think about each skill listed. Decide whether this is a skill you possess, and if you would like to use it on a job. For example, the first skill listed deals with the ability to do continuous work, that is, the same tasks many times a day, working at a steady pace. Decide if you are able to do continuous work, ask yourself if you want to. If the answer to both questions is yes, mark Item 1 "yes." If you cannot do continuous work, or prefer not to, mark Item 1 "no."

After you answer the 16 questions, turn to the following Job Matching Section. You will then be able to use the job matching section in three ways:

1. to see which jobs match your strengths and interests

2. to see what skills you have used to do the job you have been doing

3. to identify jobs that require the same skills you have used in your previous job or jobs

Specific directions for each of these uses will be given after the Skills Assessment Questionnaire.

Skills Assessment Questionnaire*

1. *Continuous*:
   On some jobs you do the same tasks many times a day and you work at a steady pace. Is this type of work for you?

   _____ Yes   _____ No

2. *Precise*:
   On some jobs there is little room for error so you must be very exact in your work. Is this type of work for you?

   _____ Yes   _____ No

3. *Using Facts*:
   On some jobs you use factual information to decide what to do. Is this type of work for you?

   _____ Yes   _____ No

4. *Working with Others*:
   On some jobs you must deal with many different people to get your work done. Is this type of work for you?

   _____ Yes   _____ No

5. *Persuading*:
   On some jobs you talk with people to try to influence other people's actions or ideas. Is this type of work for you?

   _____ Yes   _____ No

6. *Decision Making*:
   On some jobs you are responsible for making major decisions about projects, plans, and other people's duties. Is this type of work for you?

   _____ Yes   _____ No

7. *Change*:
   On some jobs you must move often from one task to another and use several different skills. Is this type of work for you?

   _____ Yes   _____ No

*The Skills Assessment Questionnaire is an adaptation of *Quest*, copyrighted by the National Career Information System, University of Oregon, 1988; used with their permission.

8. *Creative*:
   On some jobs you must express feelings and ideas in artistic ways. Is this type of work for you?

   _____ Yes   _____ No

9. *Eye-Hand Coordination*:
   On some jobs you need to be very good at handling objects quickly as you see them. Is this type of work for you?

   _____ Yes   _____ No

10. *Working with Fingers*:
    On some jobs you need to be able to do very precise work with your fingers. You need to work with small things very quickly and carefully. Is this type of work for you?

    _____ Yes   _____ No

11. *Checking Accuracy*:
    On some jobs you need to be very accurate at reading or copying written materials. You have to be very good at things like proofreading numbers and words. Is this type of work for you?

    _____ Yes   _____ No

12. *Use of Words*:
    On some jobs you need to be able to read and understand instructions easily. You have to express yourself very clearly in writing, or when talking with people. Is this type of work for you?

    _____ Yes   _____ No

13. *Use of Numbers*:
    On some jobs you need to be able to work very quickly and accurately with numbers or measurements. Is this type of work for you?

    _____ Yes   _____ No

14. *Catching on to Things:*
    On some jobs you need the ability to understand procedures and the reasonings behind them. You have to be very good at figuring out complicated things quickly and easily. Is this type of work for you?

    _____ Yes   _____ No

15. *Seeing Detail*:
On some jobs you need to be able to tell slight differences in shapes of objects and lengths of lines. You have to be able to see detail in objects, pictures, or drawings. Is this type of work for you?

_____ Yes   _____ No

16. *Physical Activity*:
Jobs require different amounts of physical activity. On some jobs you need to be very active: climbing, lifting, carrying. Is this type of work for you?

_____ Yes   _____ No

Job Matching Section

You can use the job matching section in three ways.

1. Use the job matching section to see which jobs match your strengths and interests.

   Directions: Fill in the circles at the top of each page to match your "yes" answers to the Skills Assessment Questionnaire. This is your Skills Profile. The skills used in each job have already been filled in. Go down the page, job by job, and note the number of matches between your Skills Profile and each job's skills in the first column on the left. The job or jobs with the greatest number of matches come closest to your skills. You can see a brief description of jobs that interest you in Appendix C to this book.

2. Use the section to see what skills you have used to do the job you have been doing.

   Directions: Skip down the list to the job title that comes nearest the job you have held. The skills for that job have already been filled in. These are the skills you used in carrying out that job successfully. Fill in these skills for yourself in the circles at the top of the page. Look over your answers to the Skills Assessment Questionnaire. You may have other skills that were not usually used in the job. Add these to your completed Skills Profile at the top of the page.

3. Use the sheet to identify jobs that require the same skills you have used in your previous job or jobs.

   Directions: Look down the list of job titles and identify the title or titles that come closest to jobs you have held. The skills for these jobs have already been filled in. Fill in the same circles in your Skills Profile. If you used a skill in a previous job, but prefer not to use it in a new job, do not fill in that circle. Go down the page, job by job, and note the number of matches between your Skills Profile and each job's skills in the first column on the left. The job or jobs with the greatest number of matches come closest to your skills. A checklist of jobs with brief descriptions is included in Appendix C to this book. The list provides job descriptions to help you clearly identify the work you could expect to do in each of these kinds of jobs.

Column key:
1. NUMBER OF MATCHES
2. CONTINUOUS
3. PRECISE
4. USING FACTS
5. WORKING WITH OTHERS
6. PERSUADING
7. DECISION MAKING
8. CHANGE
9. CREATIVE
10. EYE-HAND COORDINATION
11. WORKING WITH FINGERS
12. CHECKING ACCURACY
13. USE OF WORDS
14. USE OF NUMBERS
15. CATCHING ON TO THINGS
16. SEEING DETAIL
17. PHYSICAL ACTIVITY

Your Skills Profile →

Occupation	1	2	3	4	5	6	7	8	9	10	11	12	13	14	15	16
Accountants & Auditors		•	•			•					•	•	•	•		
Administrators, Educational				•	•	•					•	•	•	•	•	
Administrators, Health Services				•		•	•				•	•	•			
Administrators, Public				•		•	•				•	•	•	•	•	
Agricultural Scientists			•			•				•		•	•	•	•	
Air Traffic Controllers		•	•			•	•				•	•	•	•		
Architects				•	•			•		•	•	•	•	•		
Biologists		•	•					•	•	•	•	•	•	•		
Bookkeepers		•						•	•	•	•	•	•	•		
Business Executives				•	•	•					•	•	•			
Buyers				•	•	•	•				•	•	•	•		
Chemists		•	•			•	•		•	•	•	•		•		
Chiropractors			•	•		•			•	•		•	•	•	•	•
Claims Adjusters & Examiners			•	•							•	•	•	•		
Commercial Artists								•	•	•	•	•	•	•		
Computer Operators			•				•				•	•	•	•	•	
Computer Programmers		•	•								•	•	•	•		
Computer Repairers		•	•	•		•	•		•	•		•	•	•		
Construction Superintendents			•			•	•				•	•	•	•		
Counselors			•	•		•						•	•	•		
Dental Hygienists		•		•				•	•		•	•	•	•	•	
Dentists		•	•	•	•		•		•	•		•	•	•	•	•
Designers, Clothes		•		•					•	•	•	•	•	•		
Designers, Floral			•				•	•	•	•	•	•	•	•		
Designers, Interior				•	•	•		•	•	•	•	•	•	•		
Dietitians			•	•		•					•	•	•	•		
Dispatchers	•		•								•		•	•		
Drafters		•	•						•	•	•	•	•	•		
Ecologists		•	•			•	•		•	•	•	•	•	•		
Economists			•			•					•	•	•	•		
Electricians		•	•				•		•	•		•	•	•	•	•
Engineers		•	•			•	•		•	•	•	•	•	•		
Financial Managers			•	•		•					•	•	•	•		
Fish & Wildlife Specialists			•				•		•	•				•		•

	1 CONTINUOUS	2 PRECISE	3 USING FACTS	4 WORKING WITH OTHERS	5 PERSUADING	6 DECISION MAKING	7 CHANGE	8 CREATIVE	9 EYE-HAND COORDINATION	10 WORKING WITH FINGERS	11 CHECKING ACCURACY	12 USE OF WORDS	13 USE OF NUMBERS	14 CATCHING ON TO THINGS	15 SEEING DETAIL	16 PHYSICAL ACTIVITY
Your Skills Profile →	○	○	○	○	○	○	○	○	○	○	○	○	○	○	○	○
Foresters			•	•		•	•					•	•	•	•	
Geologists		•	•			•	•		•		•	•	•	•		
Graphic Artists							•	•	•	•	•	•	•	•		
Health & Safety Inspectors		•	•	•							•	•	•	•		
Hotel/Motel Managers			•		•	•					•	•	•	•		
Instrument Repairers		•	•						•	•	•	•	•	•		
Insurance Brokers		•	•	•					•	•	•	•	•	•	•	
Lawyers			•	•		•					•	•	•	•		
Legal Assistants		•	•	•		•					•	•	•	•		
Librarians			•			•					•	•	•	•		
Loan Officers		•	•								•	•	•	•		
Market Research Analysts		•	•								•	•	•	•		
Mathematicians		•	•								•	•	•	•		
Mechanics, Automobile		•	•			•			•	•	•			•	•	•
Mechanics, Heating & Cooling		•	•						•	•	•	•	•	•		•
Military Enlisted Personnel			•			•			•	•						•
Military Officers			•		•	•					•	•	•	•		
Nurses (LPN)		•		•		•			•	•		•		•	•	•
Nurses (RN)		•	•	•					•	•	•	•	•	•	•	•
Office Managers			•	•		•	•				•	•	•	•		
Opticians		•	•						•	•	•	•	•	•		
Optometrists			•	•					•	•	•	•	•	•		
Personnel Officers			•	•		•					•	•	•			
Pharmacists		•	•	•						•	•	•	•	•	•	
Photographers		•		•				•	•	•	•	•	•	•		
Physicians			•	•		•			•	•	•	•	•	•	•	
Physicists		•	•			•	•		•	•	•	•	•	•	•	
Pilots & Flight Engineers		•	•				•		•	•	•	•	•	•		
Production Managers			•			•	•				•	•	•	•		
Psychologists			•	•			•				•	•	•	•		
Public Relations Workers			•	•	•	•					•	•	•	•		
Purchasing Agents			•	•	•	•					•	•	•	•		
Quality Control Inspectors		•	•						•	•	•	•	•	•	•	
Radio & TV Broadcasters		•		•			•				•	•	•	•		
Real Estate Appraisers			•								•	•	•	•	•	
Real Estate Brokers			•	•							•	•	•	•	•	

Your Skills Profile →

	NUMBER OF MATCHES	CONTINUOUS	PRECISE	USING FACTS	WORKING WITH OTHERS	PERSUADING	DECISION MAKING	CHANGE	CREATIVE	EYE-HAND COORDINATION	WORKING WITH FINGERS	CHECKING ACCURACY	USE OF WORDS	USE OF NUMBERS	CATCHING ON TO THINGS	SEEING DETAIL	PHYSICAL ACTIVITY
		1	2	3	4	5	6	7	8	9	10	11	12	13	14	15	16
Receptionists		●			●							●	●		●		
Recreation Program Directors					●		●	●				●	●	●	●		
Salespeople					●	●				●		●	●	●	●		
Sales & Service Managers					●		●					●	●	●	●	●	
Sales Representatives					●	●						●	●	●	●		
Secretaries			●		●			●		●	●	●	●	●	●	●	
Social Scientists				●			●					●	●	●	●	●	
Social Workers					●	●	●						●	●	●		
Speech Pathologists					●					●	●	●	●		●	●	
Stockbrokers				●	●	●	●					●	●	●	●	●	
Surveyors			●	●			●			●	●	●	●	●	●	●	
Systems Analysts				●	●							●	●	●	●	●	
Teachers, Elementary & Secondary					●	●	●	●				●	●	●	●		
Teachers, Performing Arts					●	●	●	●	●			●	●	●	●		
Teachers, University & College					●	●	●					●	●	●	●		
Technicians, Broadcast			●	●						●	●		●	●	●		
Technicians, Dental Lab			●	●			●		●	●		●	●	●	●		
Technicians, Electronics			●	●				●		●	●	●	●	●	●	●	
Technicians, Emergency Medical				●	●					●	●	●	●	●	●	●	●
Technicians, Health			●	●	●					●	●	●	●	●	●		
Technicians, Medical Records			●		●			●				●					
Technicians, Nuclear Power			●	●				●				●	●	●	●	●	●
Technicians, Radio & TV Service			●	●				●		●	●		●	●	●	●	●
Therapists, Occupational				●				●			●	●	●	●	●		
Therapists, Physical			●	●	●	●	●			●	●	●	●	●	●		
Travel Agents					●	●						●	●	●	●		
Underwriters			●	●			●					●	●	●	●		
Urban & Regional Planners					●			●				●	●	●	●	●	
Veterinarians			●	●	●					●	●	●	●	●			●
Word Processors			●							●	●	●	●	●	●	●	
Writers & Editors					●	●			●	●		●	●	●	●	●	
Writers, Freelance									●			●			●		

Techno-Tips

The most important techno-tip is that the computer cannot be used as a shortcut to the self-examination that is necessary to really create your Building Blocks. However, it can be used to record the information. Instead of completing the forms in the book, copy them as templates and fill in the blanks directly on the computer. Completing the forms on your computer will shorten the eventual writing, rewriting, formatting, and reformatting you will carry out to create winning resumes.

Notice the plural—*resumes*. It is unlikely that you will apply for just one job and get it. (Although I do know several people who were so successful with these techniques that they did get the very first jobs for which they applied, and they were jobs the folks really wanted.) The computer gives you the power to rewrite your resume to tailor it for each job and each means of submission (electronic or otherwise). So the more information you put on the computer to start with, the better off you are.

You can create the forms with simple word processing or with a database format. If you use a database, you will want to put all the activities and experiences in one or more similar fields whether you are describing paid or unpaid work, professional or leisure activities. You will need to use a database that allows for enough characters in a field to enter lengthy narrative information. You may want to set up separate fields for different kinds of activities. For example, in one field you might list all activities related to leadership. Another field might be all responsibilities related to fiscal or financial matters. A third field might deal with client, customer, or other interpersonal relationships, and a fourth with examples of your technical expertise. Your level of computer comfort and your personal style will dictate how structured or free-form you want your Building Block entries to be.

Summary Worksheet

> *A winning resume is built step by step using the elements that employers want to see quickly and easily.*

The purpose of this chapter has been to help gather all the information you need for a winning resume. To do this, you had to examine key areas of your life so you could be more completely aware of your own skills and accomplishments.

One of the best ways to make a decision is first to look at all the possible options you have and then choose among them. Writing your resume is a series of decisions about what to tell of your work-related experiences. This chapter helped you look at the possible details you *could* include. Later chapters will help you choose which to include.

Use the checklist below to review your options.

_____ I listed all degrees, the schools at which I earned them, and the dates I attended.

_____ I listed courses of particular relevance to the job I am seeking.

_____ I listed projects or papers I completed that show job-related accomplishments.

_____ I listed school organizations in which I showed leadership.

_____ I listed honors I have earned.

_____ I listed licenses and certificates I hold.

_____ I reviewed all my jobs and wrote down my duties, skills, and accomplishments.

_____ I reviewed my experience and accomplishments in related activities, community activities, and professional organizations.

_____ I listed all papers and presentations I have given.

_____ I answered the Skills Assessment Questionnaire.

_____ I checked all dates, names, and addresses.

_____ I used the computer to organize my information.

Show and tell— use nouns and verbs

Show employers how your experience is directly connected to the job you are seeking.

Employers who were interviewed for this book said that what impresses them most in a winning resume is the forthright statement of what the job applicant has accomplished. The first thing that all the employers said they looked for was *what people had done in their previous work*. They all said that they were looking for *experience directly connected to the jobs they were trying to fill*.

In this section, you will take the statements you made about yourself in the "Building Blocks" and translate them into the words that your readers—people with the power to consider you for a job—are looking for. Two important techniques or methods are included.

The first technique involves taking your statements from sections of the Building Blocks and rephrasing them with *action words,* or *verbs.* The second technique involves your *translating your experiences into the language of job descriptions.*

A word of caution! Human beings like to see verbs. Verbs communicate action, energy. However many scanning programs are set up to look for nouns. Nouns communicate the substance of your work. These are not conflicting instructions. Every verb in your resume must have a subject *and an object*. The subject is almost always "I," although in many resume styles it remains a silent I. However, whenever you have a verb it must have something—that is, some *thing*—on which you acted. So you did not simply "analyze." You "analyzed" tax records, financial reports, student records, customer needs, building plans. I stress verbs because too often I have seen resumes that do not show enough strength. Remember, however, that like the strong person in the circus, you show your strength by how much weight you can lift. There is no lifting without weights, no verbs without objects.

Using Action Words

Action words are verbs. One way to identify a verb is by the fact that it can usually take an "ed" ending to form the past tense. Another way to identify a verb is to try to use the word "I" in front of it. A checklist of verbs in the past tense or "ed" form follows. Of course, these are not the only verbs you can use, nor will you be able to use all of them, but this list will offer very specific action words as models.

The first step is to look over the list of verbs that follows. Mentally put the word "I" in front of them. See if the verb fits a specific action or accomplishment of yours. If it does, put a pencil check next to it, or circle it, for use later.

List of Verbs

administered	carried out
advised	channeled
analyzed	collected
arranged	communicated
assembled	compiled
assumed responsibility	completed
billed	conducted
built	contacted

contracted
coordinated
counseled
created
cut
designed
determined
developed
directed
dispatched
distributed
documented
edited
established
expanded
functioned as
gathered
handled
hired
implemented
improved
inspected
interviewed
introduced
invented
maintained
managed
met with
motivated
negotiated
operated

orchestrated
ordered
organized
oversaw
performed
planned
prepared
presented
produced
programmed
published
purchased
recommended
recorded
reduced costs
referred
represented
reviewed
saved
screened
served as
served on
sold
suggested
supervised
taught
tested
trained
typed
was promoted
wrote

Rewriting Your Work History

Review the statements you made in the work history section and rewrite them to stress your actions, that is, use a verb to begin each statement.

Look over your work history for Job 1, your most recent, perhaps your present, job. Look at all the parts of the job description that you wrote: Major Duties, Special Projects, Evidence of Leadership, Evidence of Special Skills, and Company Accomplishments. Now translate that information into actions, using the verbs previously listed (and any others that you need).

EXAMPLE FROM BUILDING BLOCK C

This is information that was recorded by one resume writer in a Work History Block:

Job Title: Attorney
Employer: Self-employed
Major Duties: Diversified legal and tax practice. Outside counsel for ABC Title Co. Representative for accountants and their clients before the IRS and tax courts. Closer for several title companies.
Special Projects: Coordinator and cosponsor of a semiannual seminar for newly admitted attorneys.
Evidence of Leadership: Managed own practice.
Evidence of Special Skills: Adjunct Professor of Law and Taxation at Brooklyn Law School.
Company Accomplishments for Which I Was Responsible: All

Following is the rewritten version, using verbs. As you read it, hear how much stronger it sounds.

REWRITTEN EXAMPLE

Developed and directed diversified law and tax practice. Served as outside counsel to ABC Title Co. Conducted closings for several title companies. Represented clients and accountants before the Internal Revenue Service and tax courts. Coordinated and sponsored a semiannual seminar for newly admitted attorneys. Taught courses in Law and Taxation, as adjunct professor, at Brooklyn Law School.

As you read this, you can see that this writer decided to include teaching experience in the work history. If the writer had wished, he or she could have put that in the section for "Related Experience."

Now turn back to your Work History in Block C of Chapter 1 and rewrite each job description, beginning each statement with a verb. You can use the word "I" before each verb if you prefer.

Personal Notes

Job 1 Action Description: _____

_____

_____

_____

Job 2 Action Description: _____

_____

_____

_____

Job 3 Action Description: _____

_____

_____

_____

Job 4 Action Description: _____

_____

_____

_____

Rewriting Other Building Blocks

As you look over your personal history in the Building Blocks, you may realize that the strongest expression of your accomplishments is not in your work history, but in other areas. For example, if you are a beginning worker, your strongest accomplishments may have been in school activities. If you are trying to change careers, the most relevant experience to the new job you are seeking may have been in activities recorded in "Related Experience." If you have been a homemaker, the best expression of your skills may have been those recorded in Block F: Volunteer and Leisure Activities. All of the accomplishments and skills you recorded in those Building Blocks can and should be rewritten in the action form.

Review the list of verbs at the beginning of this section. Again, make a check next to those that you can identify with. Now go back to the Building Blocks that you completed and rewrite them in the sections provided next.

EXAMPLE FROM BUILDING BLOCK A

This example is from the Building Blocks notes of a new worker. Almost all of this applicant's experience has been in school.

Organizations and Activities: *Phoenix* (college paper)
Accomplishments: The paper was redesigned while I was managing editor. I organized a new system for reporters' assignments. I also reported all student government events before I was editor.

REWRITTEN EXAMPLE

This is the rewritten version using verbs:

Served as Managing Editor for two years, and before that as reporter. Redesigned layout of the paper. Organized and implemented an improved beat reporting system. Covered all student government events.

EXAMPLE FROM BUILDING BLOCK F

This example is from the resume of a homemaker whose major accomplishments are in volunteer activities:

Activity: Franklin Avenue Church, chair of finance committee
Areas of Accomplishment: Responsible for day-to-day operations of the church's finances, including maintenance of accounting records, payment of bills and bank reconciliations. Report frequently to church leadership and periodically to congregation. Correspond and meet with attorneys. Prepare financial statements for review by court. Currently supervising and training staff of five committee members.

REWRITTEN EXAMPLE

This is the rewritten statement, stressing action:

Managed all church finances. Maintained accounting records and prepared financial statements for review by court. Reconciled statements. Prepared and delivered oral and written reports to the church leadership and congregation. Corresponded and met with attorneys on behalf of church. Trained and supervised volunteer staff.

Personal Notes

Now rewrite information from the Building Blocks that are important to your history in the spaces provided below.

Action Rewrite 1: _____

_____

_____

_____

Action Rewrite 2: _____

_____

_____

_____

Action Rewrite 3: _____

_____

_____

_____

Action Rewrite 4: _____

_____

_____

_____

Using Job Descriptions

Every job and industry has a special *vocabulary*, or *jargon*, a way of using words, that is special to that field. Another way of catching and holding the interest of the reader of your resume is to use the words the reader expects to see.

In Appendix C you will find 100 job descriptions. Each job description contains a paragraph describing job responsibilities in specific, generally accepted terms that are in common use by corporations, government employment organizations, and other modern business institutions and another listing the skills and aptitudes required. Use the job descriptions to rewrite the material in your Building Blocks so that it captures the language of the job and field that interest you. This method of rewriting your personal history is particularly useful if you are trying to change careers, enter the job market for the first time, or develop a "portfolio career." A portfolio career enables you to take advantage of all your skills, talents, and abilities, in a variety of part-time, contractual, and consulting jobs. You can use the same experience expressed in different words to attract varied potential employers.

Another source of job descriptions is the *Occupational Outlook Handbook*, which describes virtually all the thousands of jobs in the United States. You may also want to look at one or more of the numerous books about specific fields such as *Careers in Communications, Careers in High Tech, Opportunities in Plastics Careers, Opportunities in Customer Service Careers,* or *Careers for Bookworms and Other Literary Types.* These are just a few of the hundreds of titles available to you in your library or bookstore.

In your library, school, university, or employment service office, you may also have access to a computer-based career information delivery system. These systems contain up-to-date descriptions of hundreds of occupations as well as helpful information on related training.

Finally, don't forget about the companies that you are considering in your job search. Some organizations make information such as job descriptions available for the asking. Call the personnel or human resource development office. Even better, look at the suggestions for finding information on the Internet. You will find these suggestions in this chapter's "Techno-Tips."

EXAMPLE FROM BUILDING BLOCK C

This example is from the resume of a recent college graduate. While she was in college, she held a summer job as a supervising field interviewer for a citizens' action group. This is what she wrote in her original Building Block.

I helped citizens become aware of the state legislative process and issues of toxic waste, utility control, and consumer legislation. I helped the field interviewers communicate better with the citizens. I was responsible for developing and maintaining motivation among the employees, and for supervising their work.

EXAMPLE OF A JOB DESCRIPTION

This is the job description for Public Administrator:

Responsibilities: Coordinate and direct public services to meet the needs of the nation, state, or community. Analyze problems; work with special committees and public agencies; recommend solutions to governing bodies.
Aptitudes and Skills: Ability to relate to and communicate with people; solve complex problems through analysis; plan, organize, and implement policies and programs. Knowledge of political systems; financial management; personnel administration; program evaluation; organizational theory.

REWRITTEN EXAMPLE

This is the rewritten description of the graduate's accomplishments.

Wrote pamphlets and conducted discussion groups to inform citizens of legislative processes and consumer issues. Organized and supervised crew of interviewers. Trained interviewers in effective communication skills.

EXAMPLE OF ANOTHER JOB DESCRIPTION

An individual with the same background looking for a first job as a purchasing agent or an assistant to a purchasing agent could rewrite the same experience differently. Here is the job description:

Responsibilities: Buy merchandise, materials, supplies, and equipment needed for an organization to function. Analyze needs; develop and write specifications; negotiate with salespeople.

Aptitudes and Skills: Ability to work on details; to work with people; to work easily with numbers; to write clear product specifications. Knowledge of purchasing practices; of contract, property, and insurance laws; of supplies; of pricing methods and discounts; of inventory control; of finance; of accounting.

REWRITTEN EXAMPLE

Here is the rewritten version of the same experience, tailored to fit the job description for a purchasing agent:

Organized team of field workers to promote citizen awareness of laws relating to consumer affairs. Trained interviewers in techniques for clear oral communication. Wrote specific directions for conducting interviews.

Rewriting Your Building Blocks

Rewrite your Building Blocks using the job descriptions at the back of this book. In doing this, remember to continue to use the action words discussed and listed in Method 1 of this chapter.

Job Related Rewrite 1: _____

_____

_____

_____

_____

Job Related Rewrite 2: _____

_____

_____

_____

_____

Job Related Rewrite 3: _____

_____

_____

_____

_____

Job Related Rewrite 4: _____

_____

_____

_____

_____

Techno-Tips

The techno-tips for this chapter fall into three categories. The first category is about using the Internet for information on rewriting your resume. The second category is about using the "find" capability of your word processor to shape your resume. And the third is a reminder to keep saving as you rewrite your resume entries.

As more companies list jobs on the Internet, they also provide more and more information that you—the winning resume writer—can use to shape your resume. There are several sites on the World Wide Web that list job openings and post resumes. Often the job listing tells you exactly which words to include in your resume. A recent job posting, for example, asked for "experience in all forms of popular interactive media (CD-ROM, intra-, inter-, and extra-net) and for programmers with experience in HTML, VRML, applications languages such as Director, and source code languages such as C++." If you were applying for that job, you would certainly want to include those nouns as the objects of the verbs of your work.

I hesitate to include specific job-listing sites in this book because the Internet is a much more dynamic environment than books. If I refer you to a book, you can probably find it even if the publisher is out of business and the book is out of print. It may take some looking, but the book can probably be found, particularly if it was in print when this book was published. However, once an Internet site is removed because the company running it is out of business or has changed its business, it is virtually impossible to retrieve. Having offered that caution, I will nevertheless say that http://www.careermosaic.com is, at the time of this writing, a successful, long-lived site for job listings. Another site, http://www.hotjobs.com, lists jobs in technology in more than 100 companies. The job ads from 45 (at this writing) newspapers are listed on http://www.careerpath.com. Employers seeking new college and university graduates list jobs on http://www.jobtrak.com, but this is currently available only through participating colleges. More than 600 are participating. And http://www.monster.com provides another database of jobs.

In addition to looking at job listings on an Internet site created for that purpose, you can also get information about organizations in general and, sometimes, about job vacancies by going directly to a company's web site. Many companies now include their web site addresses in all advertising. Or, if you are familiar with search engines, you can use the search engine to find the home pages and information about companies that may be of interest to you. Just remember your purpose, at this point in your resume development, it is to find the nouns and verbs, the key words that relate your work to the needs of the organization.

The *Occupational Outlook Handbook* is now available on the Internet. You can search information about occupations using an index or using job titles, key words, or occupational clusters. The address is http://stats.bls.gov/ocohome.htm.

Whether you have used the Internet or print sources to shape your experience rewrites, you can use the "find" command of your word processor to check that you have included key words. Put yourself in the place of the employer. What content is that employer looking for? Use the "find" command to search your rewrites for those key words. If they are not there, consider how to include them. For example, I was reviewing the resume of a high school science teacher. I saw lots of verbs; energy was communicated. Then I searched for "biology"—no result; "chemistry"—nothing came up; "earth science"—still nothing. That resume would never have been accepted by either a machine screening or a human reading.

Finally, remember to save all your work. I don't mean just to execute "save" commands on your computer. I mean do not overwrite your original building block material. Remember that is the raw material from which you will fashion many different resumes. Save the raw material as well as all your finished goods.

As you look over your action and job-related statements, you may feel they sound simple. Resist any impulse to change that simplicity. All of the personnel officers interviewed pulled many resumes from their files to show us statements that were so grand, they were laughable. Some examples of statements that are overdramatic or too grand will give you the idea: "A complete conceptualization with practical realization," and, "Developed keen dexterity with the panoply of tax research materials." A winning resume may evoke a smile of empathy and recognition, but it shouldn't produce a belly laugh!

Summary Worksheet

> *To build a winning resume, you need to begin by taking stock of all the experience, knowledge, and skills that you have to bring to a new job. Too many people try to begin by writing a brief statement, and never really look at all they have to offer.*

The purpose of this chapter was to help you rewrite your work and work-related experiences into the language that has the most effect in a resume.

Winning resumes use verbs to convey a strong sense of action, and also use specific vocabulary associated with the job being sought.

Use the checklist below to review.

_____ I reviewed the list of verbs on pages 34 and 35 and used as many as I could.

_____ I added some verbs to the list and used them in describing my experiences.

_____ All my experience is described in terms of action, in terms of what I did.

_____ I also rewrote the description of student activities, related experience, or volunteer work using verbs.

_____ I read the job description or descriptions that apply to my work in Appendix C.

_____ I used language from the job descriptions to highlight my skills and accomplishments at work.

_____ I kept all my rewritten descriptions simple and to the point.

_____ I included key words related to the jobs that interest me.

Assembly 3

This chapter will help you assemble all the parts you have prepared in the last two sections. First you will examine all of the essential parts of the resume and be sure that you have the necessary information for them. Then, you will take a look at the optional portions and decide which of those you would like to include. The third part of this chapter consists of sample resumes. Look them over to get a picture of how your resume may look. Finally, an outline is provided to help you draft your own resume.

Essential Parts of a Resume

The following sections *must* appear in your resume.

Heading

This section, which will go at the top of your resume, will include your name, home address, and telephone numbers. If you can receive calls at work, include your business number. This makes it easier for people to reach you during their business day. If you have an e-mail account that you check regularly, include that address as well.

Education

This section will include the information from Building Block A. If you are an experienced worker, include the degrees you have earned, the institutions at which you earned them, and the dates of attendance. List your most advanced degree first. If you have recently taken courses to upgrade or enhance your skills, include these also. Finally, if you were awarded any honors in school, these are still yours! Include them.

If you are not an experienced worker, include any unusual or particularly signficant coursework or special projects or papers that you did. The purpose of this is to show a high level of energy and/or accomplishment. If you took the regular course of study for your field, do not list your courses. One of the worst resume-writing sins all of the employers cited was the attempt to puff oneself up and to make the ordinary seem rare.

Work History

Include here the information from Building Block C and the rewritten action and job-related descriptions from Chapter 2. For each job, be sure to give your job title, your employer's name and address, and the dates of employment. Be direct and to the point. Be sure to list your most recent experience first. In general, you will also give more space to a description of your duties and accomplishments in your most recent position as well.

You will have to decide how to include company accomplishments: a good rule to follow is to include only those for which you were directly responsible. One of the personnel officers interviewed said, "It's really a turn-off when people claim full credit for achievements they were associated with, rather than those they did wholly on their own."

According to our experts, it is better *not* to include your reasons for leaving your last job on your resume. While this is important information, it is better to discuss the matter during the interview.

If you are just out of school, do show summer and part-time employment. And if your jobs were through temporary agencies, include information about both the agency and the company for which you did the work.

Professional Licenses and Certificates

This section is included if licensure or certification is required in your field. The license, issuing agency, and date of issuance should be included. See Building Block B for details. This section goes immediately before, or immediately after, your work history.

Optional Sections

The following sections are optional. As you read the descriptive material, you will see suggestions as to whether or not you should include them. In deciding, bear in mind that all the people interviewed said that conciseness and brevity were important to them in reviewing a resume. Your goal—the winning resume—should be a resume that is one or, at most, two pages long.

Related Experience

If you have work experience that does not fall neatly into your work history, this is a convenient way to show it without confusing the chronology of your resume. Look back at Building Block D to make this decision.

Professional Association Memberships and Offices Held

Only you know whether you have significant accomplishments in this sphere of activity. In most fields, work in professional associations is considered a plus in your portfolio of experience. If you filled in information in Building Block E, list that information on your resume. If your resume is getting too long, you can summarize this and just list recent highlights.

Leisure Activities

This is another truly optional section. Look over the accomplishments you listed in Block F. If you feel that what you have done in your hobbies, community activities, or volunteer work reflects energy or accomplishments that you would like the hiring official to see, include them. Remember, however, that these do not generally substitute for solid accomplishment in work, no matter how important they may have been to you or to others. If this is your main area of accomplishment, you will want to look closely at the chapter on customizing your resume. Some of the employers interviewed said that they paid no attention to this section. Others said they liked to use it to engage an applicant in conversation. (If you include any activities, you had better be prepared to talk about them. Don't try to fake it!) Still others said they thought anyone who listed hobbies needed something to fill the page. The final line of advice on leisure activities is: If you have some serious area of interest in which you have demonstrated skills or accomplishments, list it. If you have no hobbies or only passing interests, leave this section out.

Special Abilities

If you have special abilities that are valuable in your work, be sure to list them. In the computer field, these knowledges and abilities go at the start of the resume, before education. In other fields, they generally follow work history. Look back at Block G. This section is a good place to load up on nouns that describe your skills so that your resume is selected in employer key word searches.

Publications and Presentations

In completing Block H, you saw how to detail your publications and presentations. These should be included. If you happen to have written many publications and you fear a list will make your resume too long, make a simple statement within the resume, and then attach a list at the end. If this section does not apply to your accomplishments, simply omit it.

Stating Your Job Objective

There is varied opinion on the inclusion of a job objective. Some employers prefer to see it, and others see it as an item that belongs in the cover letter.

If you have a specific job objective within a field, such as tax accountant or computer operator, then the objective may be included on the resume or in the cover letter. If you are open to many jobs, do not include an objective like "a challenging position in a company with growth possibilities." This is taken for granted and does not tell the prospective employer anything new. Have you ever heard of anyone who wanted a boring position in a company destined to go nowhere? If you do not have a specific job objective, or if the objective cannot be reduced to a single clear phrase, then omit this section. Use your cover letter to state your job objective, and state it in terms related to the job you are applying for.

You must have a job objective for a scanned version of your resume or for a resume that you will submit electronically. If your resume lacks an objective, the database software may be unable to place it. Your resume will then never be seen or selected.

Summary or Highlights

The consensus among employers is that a "summary" or "highlights" section is not needed on a resume. Some of the hiring officials interviewed said that they did not care whether it was there or not, others said they preferred not to see it. One said, "I like to draw my own conclusions." Another said, "No highlights—that's what a whole resume should be. If you have to summarize the resume, you have too much in there."

References

The employers did not expect to see a list of references in a resume, but they found it helpful when it was there. One expert who found it most helpful had been in the field for many years. He said, "I know so many people in the field. I like to pick up the phone and get the true story." If you have references of people directly involved in your field, you may want to list them.

Age, Marital Status, and Physical Characteristics

It is generally better not to include this information. Formerly, some employers liked to see this personal information, and others did not. Now many employers automatically eliminate resumes that include age, marital status, or health information to avoid any possible appearance that this information may be used to discriminate in hiring.

One employer said, "Don't include these items. It's illegal to discriminate on the basis of age or marital status anyway."

Still another employer said, "I tend to eliminate resumes that have this information. If the applicant is clueless on current workplace rules, what else doesn't he or she know? I recommend omitting this information."

Sample Resumes

On the next few pages, you will find some good sample resumes. Look them over for ideas. Be sure to notice the use of action words, the direct relationship of experience to the work the applicant is hoping for. Then go to the end of this chapter to draft your own resume.

These are actual resumes of real people's work experience and backgrounds. The names, addresses, and telephone numbers have been fictionalized to protect the privacy of the people who wrote them.

Your own resume will be uniquely your own, but it will include patterns that are similar to one or more of the sample resumes. As you write the rough draft of your resume, don't be afraid to try out different wording. Write and rewrite your descriptions, and look at several different forms to see what wording you like best.

The "Techno-Tips" section of this chapter gives you suggestions and examples for reformatting to suit electronic submissions.

RESUME

Lisa Emanuel
Residence: 3300 N. Dodge
Omaha, Nebraska 68130
(402) 555-1234
Office: 1800 W. Maple
Omaha, Nebraska 68114
(402) 555-4444

DRAFTER

Job Objective—To be employed as a drafter with a large company.

Professional Experience
 Drafter—1995 to present
 Quewit Manufacturers, Omaha, Nebraska
 Completed projects on three schools, a library, a shopping mall, and other public sites.

Educational Background
 Technical Community College, Bellevue, Nebraska, enrolled in evening computer programming course (at present), expect a B.S. in 2000
 Mechanics Institute, Lincoln, Nebraska, drafting curriculum, 1993–1995
 North High School, Omaha, Nebraska, 1989–1993

Interests
 School Board No. 2, Member Curriculum Committee, 1998–present
 All sports, mountain climbing, photography

Skills
 Accuracy
 Analytical ability
 Client oriented
 High energy
 Problem solving

STEPHEN ROBBINS
FERRY ROAD
BRISTOL, RHODE ISLAND 02809
(401) 555-0029

EDUCATION: *UNIVERSITY OF RHODE ISLAND*
Bachelor of Business Administration
Expected Date of Graduation: August 1999
MAJOR: Accounting—CPA Preparation
GPA in Major: 3.5
GPA Overall: 3.2

WORK EXPERIENCE:
January 1998 to present   *ROSE & WANG, CPAs* Providence, Rhode Island
Staff Accountant:
—Prepared tax returns for corporations, partnerships, trusts, and individuals;
—Prepared clients' books and firm's workpapers for IRS tax audits;
—Organized and completed final workpaper schedules;
—Reviewed final financial statements for qualitative and quantitative errors;
—Footed totals of lines and columns on various supporting schedules.

January 1996 to   *MAKO BEARINGS INC.* Providence, Rhode Island
December 1998   Promoted to Assistant Branch Manager:
—Compiled stock orders to replace depleted inventories;
—Created system of internal controls for branch office;
—Authorized purchase orders for all back-ordered items;
—Collected receivables past due 60 days via telephone and mail correspondences;
—Determined pricing structure and published price list;
—Planned and implemented promotional sales campaign.
Order Clerk:
—Received incoming orders;
—Matched receiving reports to purchase orders, verifying accuracy;
—Acquired quotations from various vendors to fill back-ordered items.

COMPUTER SKILLS

—Able to program Visual C++;
—Academic courses in systems design and EDP Auditing;

—Detail-minded self-starter.

REFERENCES FURNISHED UPON REQUEST

Gail Freeborne
30 Spear Street
Piscataway, New Jersey 08854
(201) 555-1234

Experience
JUNE 99–PRESENT

PROMOTIONAL WRITER/EDITOR/PROOFREADER
Sea Otter Press
New Brunswick, New Jersey
Duties include: Writing press releases to promote readings, workshops, and benefits; editing manuscript submissions; proofreading promotional materials; organizing activities.

SEP 98–MAY 99

ENGLISH TUTOR
Office of Alternatives for Individual Development
Rutgers College
Tutored rhetoric and literature to referral students at the College.

SEP 96–MAY 98

NEWSPAPER REPORTER
Voice of the Students
Rutgers College
Reported campus news at the College.

SEP 95–MAY 96

PROMOTIONAL WRITER/PROOFREADER
Office of Community Services
Rutgers College
Wrote press releases to promote academic programs, guest lecturers, special workshops, and athletic events; wrote educational advertisements; proofread galleys set for print; rewrote assigned material; filed and typed.

Other Experience

SHIPPER/RECEIVER; MAIL CLERK; SUBSTITUTE TEACHER; PSYCHIATRIC AIDE; LANDSCAPER; WAITER; COOK.

Education
SEP 94–MAY 98

Rutgers College, Rutgers University
New Brunswick, New Jersey
Bachelor of Arts—English

Skills

Microsoft Word

NORA J. MCKINLAY

P.O. Box 3892   Business: (503) 555-1234
Eugene, Oregon 97403   Residence: (503) 555-4321

EXPERIENCE

PHILIP & CO. Portland, Oregon   1994 to Present

Assistant Tax Director / Senior Tax Counsel Responsible for tax research and tax planning, making recommendations and implementing them.

- Recruited, organized, and trained a professional staff of seven capable of providing effective and timely tax planning guidance.
- Increased the short- and long-term utilization of foreign tax credits in the U.S.
- Analyzed, proposed, and coordinated numerous domestic and foreign corporate reorganizations. Reviewed capital transactions of foreign subsidiary operations. Reviewed interaffiliate and third-party licensing of intangibles.

MERITRON CORP. Eugene, Oregon   1988–1994

Tax Manager Responsible for research and planning, advising management of tax opportunities.

- Reviewed U.S. consolidated tax return: prepared worldwide tax provision, handled IRS and state audits, and drafted ruling requests and protests.
- Responsible for research and planning in foreign tax credit utilization, subpart F income, foreign personal holding companies, tax haven operations, Section 482, consolidated return regulations, reorganizations, and liquidations.

PROFESSIONAL AFFILIATIONS

Attorney-at-Law admitted to practice in Oregon (1986)
CPA admitted to practice in Oregon (1989)
Tax Executives Institute
International Tax Association
American and Oregon Bar Associations
American and Oregon Societies of CPAs

EDUCATION

LL.M.   University of Oregon, Graduate Law Division (1995), major in Taxation
M.B.A. University of Oregon Graduate School of Business Administration (1988), major in Accounting
J.D.   Stanford University Law School (1985), Stanford University Scholarship
B.A.   University of Oregon (1981), major in American Civilization, Dean's List, Junior Achievement Scholarships

Martin Diamond
1342 11th Avenue
San Francisco, California 94122
Home Telephone: 415-555-1234
Office Telephone: 415-555-4982
E-mail: martdi@xyz.com

HARDWARE: IBM RS 6000
SOFTWARE: IBM AIX, Oracle
LANGUAGES: C, Visual C++, Visual BASIC

EXPERIENCE

Estimable Life Insurance Company   1989–present
San Francisco, California

PROJECT LEADER   1995–present
Developed systems including: Deficiency Reserve Evaluation; Mortality and
Termination Experience Studies; Agent Performance Analysis; and Retirement Plan
and Bonuses.
Led a team of programmers and consultants to develop and implement the com-
pany's reinsurance systems including conversion, maintenance, automatic billing, on-
line transaction generation, policy exhibit, and management reports.
Supervised a team of 15 professionals.

SENIOR PROGRAMMER/ANALYST   1991–1995
Developed and implemented company's declared dividend scale calculation, update,
and dividend liability systems.
Improved and maintained actuarial, reinsurance, and general agents commission
payment systems.
Converted premium rates, cash values, reserve, and dividends to LIFE-COMM
systems.

PROGRAMMER/ANALYST   1989–1991
Responsible for various projects designed to calculate premium rates, values,
reserves, and dividends.
Developed general agents commission payment system.
Participated in developing new product premium rates, cash values, and dividends.

EDUCATION

San Francisco State College, B.S. (cum laude), 1989, Major: mathematics; Minor:
    computer systems.

The Resume: First Draft

Using the outline provided in the next few pages, create a first draft of your resume. Use the material you developed in the Building Blocks and the Action and Job-Related Rewrites. Use the ideas you got from looking over the sample resumes. In the outline, you will see space for all of the optional sections. Before including any of these, you may want to reread the notes on optional sections given earlier in this chapter.

In the outline, headings that should be part of the finished product are in bold type, for example: **Education**. Items that are to be filled in *by you*, eliminating the word as a heading, are indicated by parentheses, for example: (Name). All *optional* items are marked with an asterisk, for example: Honors*. To review the reasons for including one or more of the optional sections see pages 49 to 52.

Personal Notes

First Draft Resume Form

(Name) _____

(Address) _____

(City, State, Zip Code) _____

(Home Telephone) _____

(Office Telephone) _____

(E-mail) _____

Objective* _____
　　　　　　(State a job objective only if it is specific.)

Education *(Put this at the end of your resume if you are an experienced worker.)*

(Diploma, Certificate, or Degree) _____ (Dates) _____

(Institution) _____

(Major or Area of Concentration) _____

(Diploma, Certificate, or Degree) _____ (Dates) _____

(Institution) _____

(Major or Area of Concentration) _____

Experience

(Job Title) _____ (Dates) _____

(Employer) _____

(Duties and Accomplishments) _____

_____

_____

(Job Title) _____ (Dates) _____

(Employer) _____

(Duties and Accomplishments) _____

_____

(Repeat as needed on scrap paper. Be sure to list your most recent experiences first and work backward.)

Licenses and Certification

(License) _____ (Dates) _____

(Issuing Agency) _____

(License) _____ (Dates) _____

(Issuing Agency) _____

Related Work Experience*

(Job Title) _____ (Dates) _____

(Employer) _____

(Duties and Accomplishments) _____

_____

(Repeat as often as needed.)

Honors*

_____

_____

Interests and Hobbies*

_____

_____

Special Abilities/Considerations*

_____

_____

(List fluency in foreign languages, computer skills, availability for travel, etc.)

Publications and Presentations*

_____

_____

References*

(Name) _____

(Title) _____

(Organization) _____

(Address) _____

(Telephone Number) _____

(Name) _____

(Title) _____

(Organization) _____

(Address) _____

(Telephone Number) _____

Techno-Tips

There are four major ways, other than mailing a printed copy, in which you can use technology to submit your resume, and each method calls for a somewhat different technique. For each technique, there is a section within these Techno-Tips.

- You can submit your printed resume by fax directly to an employer or to an agency working on behalf of the employer. Whether you mail or fax your resume, you may want to assume that it will be scanned into a database for further use. The section "Creating a Scannable Resume" tells you how to format your resume for scanning.

- You can send your resume by e-mail as an attached file. The section "Sending Your Resume by E-Mail" tells you how to accomplish this.

- You can list your resume on a resume-listing service on the Internet, either in response to a job listing on the Web or to self-advertise. The section "Using a Web-Based Resume Listing Service" tells how to create the on-line resume.

- You can create your own Web page to attract prospective employers. "A Few Words on Your Web Page Resume" is a brief section about creating a Web page of your own as a way of distributing your resume and attracting employers.

Each of the methods of submitting your resume calls for different techniques of layout, general style, and even the choice of words. You will find the details of these techniques in the four sections that follow.

In addition, in each section, I provide examples of how to change your resume to maximize the utility of the technique. To do this, I have taken some of the sample resumes you saw earlier in this chapter and recast them to fit the technology under discussion. You will need to do the same thing. You may very well have several versions of your resume, not just different versions for different employers or jobs, but different versions to take advantage of scanning, e-mail, and resume-listing services.

Creating a Scannable Resume

What is scanning? What should I change to make my resume scannable? What will my scannable resume look like? Depending upon your experience with computers, these are questions you may be asking as you begin reading this section. We begin with some basics, but if you know these, just skip right to the part that tells you what to do.

Scanners are often attached to computers to enter data quickly from print to images that the computer can read. After the image is read into the computer, optical character recognition (OCR) software looks at the image and translates what it sees into letters and numbers. Then other software is used to identify important information about you such as your name and address, your work history, your experience and skills.

OCR software is imperfect, or perhaps, too perfect. When it is looking for matches between the images you have supplied and letters and numbers, it can only translate what it sees against the set of characters it has been given. If it has been given asterisks, for example, and you use bullets to highlight different responsibilities, unlike a human, it cannot think, "Oh yes, this person has used bullets." Instead, it will try to match your bullets against some character, perhaps periods, thereby creating strange sentences indeed. It may not recognize or be able to translate italics or underlining. Parentheses may be misinterpreted as part of the letter they adjoin or as some other symbol. Smudges may become characters and broken letters may be omitted altogether.

Once the resume has been scanned, other software is used to place it in your potential employer's database and then to search it for the key words that the employer has identified for the job you are seeking. While there are a number of different programs for scanning and searching, the rules to increase your chances are generally the same.

The rules for creating a scannable resume are fairly simple. In fact, that is the primary rule: *Keep it simple*. Here are ten pointers to show you how to write a winning scannable resume.

1. Use white, 8½" × 11" paper, printed on one side only.

2. Use a standard font such as Arial, Optima, Universe, Times New Roman, or Courier in 12 point typeface. Do not condense or expand the type.

3. Avoid all "fancy" type—no italics, underlining, boxes, graphics, bullets, or columns. Do use capital letters and line spacing to help organize your resume.

4. Be sure to put each of the following on separate lines: name, address, phone number, fax number, and e-mail address. Put your name only at the top of each additional page.

5. Use a structured resume format, with clear headings, such as those we have suggested throughout this book.

6. Increase your use of key words, particularly nouns and industry jargon, to increase your chances that the key word search will select your resume.

7. Be sure to print your resume on a laser or ink jet printer. Dot matrix print and less-than-perfect photocopies do not scan well.

8. Do not staple or fold your resume. Either of these can make marks that will "confuse" the OCR software. Mail it in a large enough, protective envelope.

9. Faxing often reduces the quality of an image. If you must fax your resume, set the fax machine on "fine" rather than "standard" mode, and, if possible, follow with a mailed copy.

10. If you are uncertain whether your resume will be scanned or read, ask the employer. If you cannot do that, you may want to send two copies with Post-It Notes attached, one indicating "scannable resume," and the other marking the "hard copy resume."

There are five resumes earlier in this chapter. The last one, for Martin Diamond, needs no changes to be scannable. The restructured resumes for the other four job applicants follow. You will see that they look quite alike. That is because the structure that is successful in scanning allows for less creativity in appearance and relies more upon words.

Lisa Emanuel
3300 N. Dodge
Omaha, NE 68130
402 555-1234
emanuel@xyz.edu

OBJECTIVE
Drafter for public and large private design and construction

EXPERIENCE
Drafter, Quewit Manufacturers, Omaha, Nebraska, 1995 to present
Completed projects on three schools, library, shopping mall, and other public sites
Team member of drafting-engineering-construction team

EDUCATION
Technical Community College, Bellevue, Nebraska, enrolled in evening computer
programming course. Expect B.S. in 2000.
Mechanics Institute, Lincoln, Nebraska, Drafting certificate, 1993 to 1995
North High School, Omaha, Nebraska, 1989 to 1993

INTERESTS
Member Curriculum Committee, School Board 2, 1998 to present
Team sports, mountain climbing, photography

SKILLS
Accuracy, analytical ability, client oriented, high energy, problem solving

STEPHEN ROBBINS
FERRY ROAD
BRISTOL, RI 02809
401 555-0029
SAR@XYZ.COM

EDUCATION
University of Rhode Island, BBA, Accounting, CPA Preparation, GPA in major of 3.5. Expected graduation date of 1999.

OBJECTIVE
Tax accountant

WORK EXPERIENCE

STAFF ACCOUNTANT, Rose & Wang, CPAs, Providence, RI, 1998 to present.
Prepared tax returns for corporations, partnerships, trusts, and individuals;
Prepared clients' books and firm's workpapers for IRS tax audits;
Organized and completed final workpaper schedules;
Reviewed final financial statements for qualitative and quantitative errors;
Footed totals of lines and columns on various supporting schedules.

ASSISTANT BRANCH MANAGER, Mako Bearings, Inc., Providence, RI, 1996 to 1998
Promoted from Order Clerk;
Compiled stock orders to replace depleted inventories;
Created system of internal controls for branch office;
Authorized purchase orders for all back-ordered items;
Collected receivables past due 60 days via telephone and mail correspondence;
Determined pricing structure and published price list;
Planned and implemented promotional sales campaign.
As ORDER CLERK:
Received incoming orders;
Matched receiving reports to purchase orders, verifying accuracy;
Acquired quotations from various vendors to fill back-ordered items.

SKILLS
Programming in Visual C++
Academic courses in systems design and EDP auditing
Detail-minded self-starter

REFERENCES furnished upon request.

Gail Freeborne
30 Spear Street
Piscataway, NJ 08854
201 555-1234

OBJECTIVE
Reporter

EDUCATION
English Major, Rutgers College, Rutgers University, BA, 1994 to 1998

RELEVANT EXPERIENCE
PROMOTIONAL WRITER, EDITOR, AND PROOFREADER
Sea Otter Press, New Brunswick, New Jersey, June 1999 to present
Writing press releases promoting events including readings, workshops, and community benefits
Editing manuscript submissions
Proofreading promotional materials
Organizing community activities

ENGLISH TUTOR
Office of Alternatives for Individual Development, Rutgers College, Sept. 1998 to May 1999
Tutoring writing and reading skills to referral students at the College

NEWSPAPER REPORTER
Voice of the Students, Rutgers College Newspaper, Sept. 1996 to May 1998
Reporting local and campus news

OTHER EXPERIENCE
Shipper and Receiver; Mail Clerk; Substitute Teacher; Psychiatric Aide; Landscaper; Waiter; Cook

SKILLS
Word processing
MS Word
Willing to travel
Follow through
Open communication

NORA J. MCKINLAY
P.O. Box 3892
Eugene, OR 97403
Home Telephone: 503-555-4321
Office Telephone: 503-555-1234

OBJECTIVE
Senior Tax Counsel

EDUCATION
LL.M., University of Oregon, Graduate Law Division, Taxation Major, 1995
MBA University of Oregon, Graduate School of Business Administration,
Accounting Major, 1988
JD Stanford University Law School, Stanford University Scholarship, 1985
BA University of Oregon, American Civilization Major, Dean's List, Junior
Achievement Scholarships, 1981

EXPERIENCE

ASSISTANT TAX DIRECTOR/SENIOR TAX COUNSEL, Philip & Co, Portland
OR, 1994 to present
Tax research, tax planning, making and implementing recommendations for
company growth.
Recruiting, organizing, training professional staff of seven, capable of providing
effective and timely tax planning guidance.
Increasing short- and long-term utilization of foreign tax credits in the U.S.
Analyzing, proposing, and coordinating numerous domestic and foreign corporate
reorganizations.
Reviewing capital transactions of foreign subsidiary operations.
Reviewing interaffiliate and third-party licensing of intangibles.

TAX MANAGER, Meritron Corp., Eugene, OR, 1988–1994
Reviewed U.S. consolidated tax returns: prepared worldwide tax provision, handled IRS and state audits, and drafted ruling requests and protests.
Researched and planned foreign tax credit utilization, subpart F income, foreign
personal holding companies, tax haven operations, Section 482, consolidated
return regulations, reorganizations, liquidations.

PROFESSIONAL AFFILIATIONS
Attorney-at-Law admitted to practice in Oregon 1986
CPA admitted to practice in Oregon 1989
Tax Executives Institute
International Tax Association
American and Oregon Bar Associations
American and Oregon Societies of CPAs

Sending Your Resume by E-Mail

You may want to send your resume by e-mail because that is what you have been requested to do by the employer whose ad you are answering. You may have found that ad in one of the traditional sources, such as the newspaper, or by going to the Web home page of companies that interest you. More and more companies, particularly those in the high-tech field, list job openings right on their own web sites.

If you use e-mail, you probably are aware of the limited ability you have to format the material you are sending. In addition, depending upon the program the other party has, the e-mail may arrive with even less style than you included. Although communication by e-mail across the Internet improves almost day-by-day, it is still difficult for you to know how well the page you send will resemble the page your potential employer receives. Very often, the first page of your e-mail is taken up by the header that contains a raft of information about the machine-to-machine transmission of your letter. If you send your resume by e-mail, the only thing the employer receives on the first screen may be your name. In addition, employers who want to print your resume or store it in a database must find where it begins and separate that from the unneeded header.

You can exercise some control over the appearance of your e-mailed resume by sending it as an attached file to your e-mail rather than as a part of the e-mail itself. Because you have no way of knowing which word processing program your potential employer has, the best way to ensure compatibility of sending and receiving is to send your resume as an ASCII file. ASCII (pronounced *askee)* is a simple form of text recognized by virtually all computer platforms (for example, both Windows and Macintosh) and all computer applications of interest to us. ASCII stands for American Standard Code for Information Interchange.

Without getting into technicalities of binary coding, we can explain that one of the reasons that ASCII works is because it is used to communicate in text that has no frills and virtually no formatting. Remember the rule for scannable resumes was *keep it simple*. The rule for ASCII text is *keep it simpler*. You can use all of the resume ideas you used in developing your scannable resume with a few additional pointers. Here are the ten pointers to show you how to write a winning e-mailed resume.

1. Use a standard font such as Arial, Optima, Universe, Times New Roman, or Courier in 12 point typeface. Do not condense or expand the type.

2. Avoid all "fancy" type—no italics, underlining, boxes, graphics, bullets, or columns. Do use capital letters and line spacing to help organize your resume.

3. Do not use any centering. Keep all text left-justified, straight on the left margin.

4. The computer programs that will read your resume prefer simple left-justified text. However, if you want to indent, do not use a tab key, rather, type in the number of spaces you want.

5. Be sure to put each of the following on separate lines: name, address, phone number, fax number, and e-mail address. Put your name only at the top of each additional page.

6. Use a structured resume format, with clear headings, such as those we have suggested throughout this book.

7. Increase your use of key words, particularly nouns and industry jargon, to increase your chances that the key word search will select your resume.

8. Before you send your resume, save it in "text only" mode. On most programs, this is called "rich text format" or RTF. Often, you will have to save your resume file and close it before you can attach it to an e-mail message.

9. Of course, you will not be printing your resume and sending it. You will be transmitting by e-mail, so you need not worry about paper and print quality. However, you should print a copy of your resume to see what it looks like *before* you send it. In the next chapter, you will read about proofreading and checking your resume. All of that should be done, before you hit the fateful "send" button.

10. Then, when you are sending your e-mail response, direct the attention of the reader to the attached file. Be sure to find out how to attach a file in the e-mail

program you are using. In most cases, there is a button or pull-down menu within e-mail that lets you attach a file. Once you find and activate it, the program prompts you for the name and location of the file you are using. For example, in the version of Eudora that I use, within the Message menu, there is a command to "Attach File." Once I click on that, the directory of all my files comes on the screen. I scroll through the directories and subdirectories to find the file I want to attach, click on it, and the job is done. Hit the "send" button and your resume is gone. Just be sure you are ready to send it before you do so.

For examples of how to set up ASCII or RTF, look at any of the resumes in the "Creating a Scannable Resume" section. Just left-justify the headings instead of centering them and you have a resume you can save in RTF. You may also want to create a more traditional, print version of your resume to bring with you when your winning resume gets you the job interview.

Using a Web-Based Resume Listing Service

The World Wide Web contains more and more services to help the job hunter. And you want to be able to take advantage of all of those that will be of particular help to you. In some fields, employers are making increasing use of resume listing services. Both potential employers and job seekers have their space in these services. Job seekers like you can list their resumes in categories or fields of work that are of interest to them, hoping that a prospective employer searching the list will select their resume. Potential employers list jobs hoping that the best candidates will post their resumes to them.

You can take advantage of both types of services. Once you have a resume listing service that includes jobs of the type that interest you, you can post your resume as a type of "Job Wanted" ad, and you can also respond to job listings you see. The only difference in what you actually do is that if you are responding to a job listing, you indicate the number or other identifier of that job.

Two companies that are heavily involved in the resume listing business are RESTRAC and RESUMIX. The address or URL of the first is http://www.restrac.com and the URL of the second is http://www.resumix.com. You can find other resume listing services that serve your field by using one of the search engines such as www.infoseek.com, www.hotbot.com, or www.dogpile.com. In the search box, put the name of the job and the word *resumes*. For example, enter "sales resumes" or "accountant resumes" and then carry out the search. You will probably not only get what you want, but you can sort through the listings you receive for resume services in your field.

The resume listing services generally provide forms that you fill in and that they then format to fit their database. The skills you used in creating your scannable resume and your e-mailed resume are useful in knowing how to write your winning resume listing resume. You will need to be brief and to the point, stress skills, and work within a framework. You will note that the forms ask you to use a "carriage return" as you enter information. That is because you are using ASCII format and you want to be sure to stay within the vertical and horizontal sides of the box provided.

A word of caution. Some people prefer not to put their home addresses and telephone numbers on the Web. Remember, just as you can get to the site to list your resume and look at those of others, so can others get to your resume. Once you have put your address and telephone number on the Web, there's no way to recall the information. Some people will list their city, state, and e-mail address. Some prefer to list only their e-mail address and to include the location of the work they are seeking in the objective box. On the other hand, some resume listing services require your address to be sure that you are on the up-and-up. If you do list any identifying information, be sure that you are cautious in setting up any meetings or giving any further information in response to queries. I am not suggesting that you hide. I am suggesting that you verify any further requests for information to be sure they are coming from a potential employer and not a prankster.

Following is an example of a blank form, and then an example of the same form completed for sample resume of Stephen Robbins. You will see that some information that was in the resume has no place in the form and that other information, such as dates of employment, needs to be supplied in greater detail.

Sample Resume Listing Form

Name _____

Home Address _____

City _____ State _____ Zip _____

Work Address _____

City _____ State _____ Zip _____

Home Phone Number _____

Work Phone Number _____

Fax Number _____

E-Mail Address _____

OBJECTIVE (Type of Employment Sought) (Please use carriage returns.)

```



```

EDUCATION

School _____ Major _____

Degree _____ Year of Graduation _____ GPA _____

School _____ Major _____

Degree _____ Year of Graduation _____ GPA _____

School _____ Major _____

Degree _____ Year of Graduation _____ GPA _____

School _____ Major _____

Degree _____ Year of Graduation _____ GPA _____

EMPLOYMENT HISTORY

Employer _____

Job Title _____

From (mm/yy) _____ **To (mm/yy)** _____

Description of Duties (Please use carriage return.)

```
┌──────────────────────────────────────────────────────────┐
│                                                          │
│                                                          │
│                                                          │
│                                                          │
│                                                          │
└──────────────────────────────────────────────────────────┘
```

Employer _____

Job Title _____

From (mm/yy) _____ **To (mm/yy)** _____

Description of Duties (Please use carriage return.)

```
┌──────────────────────────────────────────────────────────┐
│                                                          │
│                                                          │
│                                                          │
│                                                          │
│                                                          │
└──────────────────────────────────────────────────────────┘
```

Employer _____

Job Title _____

From (mm/yy) _____ **To (mm/yy)** _____

Description of Duties (Please use carriage return.)

```
┌──────────────────────────────────────────────────────────┐
│                                                          │
│                                                          │
│                                                          │
│                                                          │
│                                                          │
└──────────────────────────────────────────────────────────┘
```

Employer _____

Job Title _____

From (mm/yy) _____ **To (mm/yy)** _____

Description of Duties (Please use carriage return.)

```



```

Employer _____

Job Title _____

From (mm/yy) _____ **To (mm/yy)** _____

Description of Duties (Please use carriage return.)

```



```

Additional Information (skills, abilities, etc.) (Please use carriage return.)

```



```

Sample Resume Listing Form—Completed for Stephen Robbins

Name Stephen Robbins

Home Address Ferry Road

City Bristol   **State** RI   **Zip** 02809

Work Address

City   **State**   **Zip**

Home Phone Number 401 555-0029

Work Phone Number

Fax Number

E-Mail Address SAR@XYZ.COM

OBJECTIVE (Type of Employment Sought) (Please use carriage return.)

Tax accountant in Rhode Island or Massachusetts

EDUCATION

School University of Rhode Island   **Major** Accounting, CPA Preparation

Degree BBA   **Year of Graduation** 1999   **GPA** 3.5

School   **Major**

Degree   **Year of Graduation**   **GPA**

School   **Major**

Degree   **Year of Graduation**   **GPA**

School   **Major**

Degree   **Year of Graduation**   **GPA**

EMPLOYMENT HISTORY

Employer Rose & Wang, CPAs

Job Title Staff Accountant

From (mm/yy) 12/98   **To (mm/yy)** 01/00

Description of Duties (Please use carriage return.)

Prepared tax returns for corporations, partnerships, trusts, and individuals;
Prepared clients' books and firm's workpapers for IRS tax audits;
Organized and completed final workpaper schedules;
Reviewed final financial statements for qualitative and quantitative errors.

Employer Mako Bearings, Inc.

Job Title Assistant Branch Manager

From (mm/yy) 01/97   **To (mm/yy)** 12/98

Description of Duties (Please use carriage return.)

Compiled stock orders to replace depleted inventories;
Created system of internal controls for branch office;
Authorized purchase orders; Collected receivables;
Determined pricing structure; Planned and implemented sales campaign.

Employer Mako Bearings, Inc.

Job Title Order Clerk

From (mm/yy) 03/96   **To (mm/yy)** 01/97

Description of Duties (Please use carriage return.)

Received incoming orders;
Matched receiving reports to purchase orders, verifying accuracy;
Acquired quotations from various vendors to fill back-ordered items.

Employer

Job Title

From (mm/yy)   **To (mm/yy)**

Description of Duties (Please use carriage return.)

```



```

Employer _____

Job Title _____

From (mm/yy) _____ **To (mm/yy)** _____

Description of Duties (Please use carriage return.)

```



```

ADDITIONAL INFORMATION (skills, abilities, etc.) (Please use carriage return.)

```
Programming in Visual C++
Academic courses in systems design and EDP auditing
Detail-minded self-starter
```

A Few Words on Your Web Page Resume

You can use the most sophisticated tools of the Internet, including multimedia and links to other parts of the Web, to create your own Web page as an advertisement for your services. The techniques for creating such a Web page are beyond the scope of this book, but if you are even considering doing this, you probably have some of the skills necessary. However, a word or two of caution so that you know how to write a winning Web page resume.

1. Remember the purpose of the resume is to get you a job interview. Restrict your information to that which serves the purpose.

2. Consider that if you send your readers off on links to other parts of the World Wide Web, you may never

see them again. Consider how any links contribute to *you* getting a job.

3. Be sure to make your information accessible. Consider how a potential employer will know that your web site is out there advertising your services.

4. Do not include every graphic or auditory feature you can dream up. Do include those that demonstrate that you are the best person for the job you are seeking.

Summary Worksheet

> The most impressive information on a winning resume is the description of what the applicant has accomplished on previous jobs. Hiring officials are looking for experience directly connected with the jobs they are trying to fill.

The purpose of this chapter has been to help you choose the experiences and details that best show your educational and work history and your skills and accomplishments.

In Chapter 1 you wrote out and reviewed everything you could possibly use in your resume. In this chapter you made the hard decision about what to include and what to leave out.

Use the checklist below to review your decisions.

_____ I have included information for the essential parts of a resume.

    _____ Heading (Name, Address, Telephone Number)

    _____ Education

    _____ Work History

    _____ Certificates and Licenses

_____ I have read the information about optional sections.

_____ I have thought about my own experience and the job I am applying for in deciding about including optional sections.

_____ I have included optional sections that show something strong in my experience.

_____ I have left out optional sections that would just be page fillers.

_____ I have a first draft of my resume.

_____ I have compared it to one or more of the sample resumes.

_____ I have added or taken out some information.

_____ I like my resume so far.

_____ I can format my resume for scanning or e-mailing.

_____ I know how to use the forms of a resume listing service.

Getting physical

> *Use the layout of your resume to draw attention to its most important facts.*

In this chapter, you will use the draft of your resume, which you created in the last chapter, and produce a finished printed copy. First, we will discuss ideas on layout and spacing. Then suggestions on typing, paper, and reproduction are provided. Finally, there is a section to help you with proofreading your resume.

The personnel officers and hiring officials interviewed for this book stated clearly that there is no one style or paper that is preferable. What emerged from their comments is the *overwhelming importance of neatness and "good grooming" in a resume.* Some of the worst sins that they objected to in resume presentation are sloppiness, misspellings, thumb smudges, hand corrections, whiting-out. One employer summed it up this way, "A piece of paper that has not been taken care of shows disdain for the reader, the process, and the job applicant himself." Others said that, since attention to detail was important to their fields, lack of attention to details in the resumes showed them that the applicants could probably not do the job at hand.

Organization that is easy to read and clarity of presentation are the two other factors to consider in preparation.

Layout for Printed Resumes

There is no single appropriate layout that will fit every resume, but there are some good rules to follow.

First, leave at least a one-inch margin all around the page to frame the information.

Second, use spacing between lines and indentations of material to draw attention to important facts. Do not cram everything together.

Third, be consistent in the type of headings you use. For example, if you capitalize the heading EDUCATION, do not use initial capital letters and underlining for the equal heading Job Experience.

Finally, try to fit your resume onto one page. If this is not possible, try to arrange your material so that the most important items appear on page one.

All of the resumes given as examples in Chapter 3 are also examples of good layouts. Following are three examples of resumes with *poor* layouts. As you examine each resume, try to identify the major layout errors.

EXAMPLE: PROBLEM RESUME NO. 1

PAUL C. MICHAELS

2121 Sumac Street
Champaign, Ill. 61821

Messages &
Home: (217)
555-0852
555-1457

Business:
(217)
555-8400
Ext. 304

Auditor
Building Service Pension & Health Funds
Chicago, Illinois
September, 1996–Present
Responsibility: Autonomous audits
of contributing employers
Microsoft Office Suite experience

Analyst
FairViews
Chicago, Illinois
May, 1995–Present
(Hobby)

M.B.A.
Seton Hall University, So. Orange, N.J. 07079
January, 1994–May, 1995
G.P.A.: 3.57
Concentration: Quantitative Analysis

Accountant
Bandlor-Hall, Inc.
Chicago, Illinois
September, 1990–January, 1994
Charges: Computerized financial statements,
bank reconciliations, and journal entries.

B.S.
Seton Hall University, May, 1992
1988–December, 1991
Major: Accounting
Minor: Journalism

Accounting Clerk
Building Service Pension & Health Funds
Summers 1987–1995
Various bookkeeping duties.

References will be furnished upon request.

EXAMPLE: PROBLEM RESUME NO. 2

MARK E. RUCZINSKI
4330 Chesapeake NW
Washington, D.C. 20010

PERSONAL:

Born: May 10, 1963
Married with two children
Height 6'2"
Weight 160 lbs.

EDUCATION:

1991–1993	Pace University School of Law, White Plains, New York J.D. Received June 1994
1987–1989	Iona College Graduate School of Business, New Rochelle, New York
	Masters degree in Business Administration in Accounting, received in June 1989
1978–1985	Iona College, New Rochelle, New York
	Bachelor of Business Administration received in Finance June 1978; member of Dean's Honor List, last four semesters; Received scholarship to Iona College Graduate School of Business.

PROFESSIONAL QUALIFICATIONS:

Admission to New York Bar—1994
Certified Public Accountant—New York 1990
Member of the American Institute of Certified Public Accountants
Member of the New York Society of Certified Public Accountants

BUSINESS EXPERIENCE:

1992 to Present	Greyhound Bus Lines, Inc. New York, New York
	Assistant General Counsel and Assistant to Treasurer
	Responsibilities include tax research and planning for the corporation and its subsidiaries, legal research, and writing.
1985–1992	City of Washington, Department of Finance, Washington, D.C.
	Assistant to Financial Analyst
	Responsibilities included financial analysis and preparation of financial reports including the annual financial report and financial schedules for bond prospectus.

EXAMPLE: PROBLEM RESUME NO. 3

John Lee
3310 15th Street
San Francisco, California 94114
Telephone: (415) 555-1687

PROFESSIONAL OBJECTIVE:	An entry level position in the field of accounting leading to managerial responsibilities.

EDUCATION: January, 1998	Master of Science	
	San Francisco State University	San Francisco, California
	Majoring in Accounting.	
	Program included independent study of Advanced Accounting Theory, Financial Statements Analysis. Special Interest in Tax Law.	
	42 semester hour program completed.	
	Q.P.R. 3.0 on 4.0 scale.	
	Thesis: Impacts of Economic Recovery Tax of 1981 on Investment.	
1994–1996	Stanford University	Palo Alto, California
	Completed 60 credits of Business Core Courses.	
	Accounting. Q.P.R. 3.0 on 4.0 scale.	
1994	Bachelor of Arts	
	University of San Francisco	San Francisco, California
	Majoring in Psychology.	
	Activities: President of Student Drama Club.	
	Successfully produced five plays.	
WORK HISTORY SUMMARY: 1992–1997	5-years retail experience . . . Cash responsibilities . . . Assisted management in shipping. Self-funded 100% of education.	
PERSONAL:	Determined, strong-willed, hard-working, single. Excellent health. Permanent legal resident.	
REFERENCES:	Available upon request.	

Problem Resume 1 has several major problems in layout. First, *the order of items is confusing.* There are two jobs listed, then an educational degree, followed by a third job, and another degree. Although you do want to follow a chronological order, the order should be within major categories, such as Education and Job Experience.

A second problem is related to the first. *There are no section headings to help the reader through the flow of information.*

Margins are a third problem. While you do want to allow sufficient white space to create an open look, this resume has too much of a good thing.

Finally, looking beyond the layout at the words, *notice the absence of an action-oriented description of job duties and accomplishments.* A reader gets the feeling that the wide margins are there to make up for an absence of content. The resume looks very formal at first glance, but it is hard to follow, and gives little information.

The major problem with Problem Resume 2 is poor judgment. The first poor judgment consists of including the *inappropriate personal information.* The second poor judgment is about *order.* While there are neat headings and the resume is easy to read, the information least relevant to the job appears first. Put yourself in the place of the resume reader. The reader is looking for someone to fill a specific job. Unless that reader is looking for a model or a bouncer, physical qualifications are least important, yet that information comes first. A second problem is the *excessive space given to the bare bones information under education.* The numerous lines of information could be reduced to three or four by using a different format: "J.D., Pace University School of Law, 1988." It is not necessary to give the location of a college unless it would be generally unknown. Because so much space is given to meaningless educational detail, the two honors received are just about lost by the reader. These should be in a special section headed *Honors,* placed between *Education* and *Professional Qualifications.*

Notice how the layout of Problem Resume 3 calls most attention to the *location* of activities, rather than the *accomplishments* themselves. Notice also how breaking up lines incorrectly makes it almost impossible to figure out what the writer is trying to say, unless you pay close attention and give the resume a lot of time. No personnel officer reading dozens of resumes will do that. As to content, this resume is an example of a poor use of the job objective. It should simply have been left out.

Remember that the layout of your resume should accomplish three important things. It should be clearly organized, so the reader can see quickly what is included. It should emphasize what is most important. It should be neat and attractive to look at, without drawing attention away from the information.

Layout for Your Own Resume

Take the draft of your resume and work on a layout. Check the arrangement to see that the areas you think will be most important to the reader appear early in the resume. If the resume is getting too cluttered, try to eliminate some of the optional areas, or try to reduce the detail in your earliest job descriptions. You will probably have to try several layouts before you are pleased with the results. You may want to have a friend read over the resume for clarity of presentation and balance.

Ask your friend to tell you what impresses her or him as most important. Make sure that this is the information that you want to emphasize. If it isn't, make changes to correct it.

Be sure that you use most of the space for the most important information. Allow space between each block of information so each one is easy to spot on the page.

Production and Reproduction

A resume should be word processed and printed on good quality bond paper, either white or ivory. All of the employers that we interviewed said that they were not impressed by professionally designed resume layouts. In fact, several of our experts made the point that they *preferred a straightforward standardized resume without any special typographical effects.* They felt that overdone resumes indicated that the applicant had been "packaged," and was not presenting facts about herself or himself so much as presenting a fancy image.

After the resume has been printed, and you have carefully proofread it, you may want to have it commercially reproduced. Quality reproduction does count. You do not want to have a carefully written, organized, and typed resume marred with copy machine smudges. If you reproduce it yourself, be sure you use a clean machine and the same quality paper on which the original was typed. If you have it done by a copy service, be sure the person understands what you want. Ask for a sample of paper and reproduction quality before you place your order. On the other hand, the power and ease of computers enables you to prepare a slightly different resume for each job and print it yourself on a high-quality laser or inkjet printer.

One question that often comes up is whether you should use any special calligraphy or designs to draw attention to your resume. The experts' answer to this question was unanimous. Unique typing and layout should be used only when the applicant is applying for a job in which design ability or artistic qualities are important. Then the resume often serves as an example of the person's work. If you are an applicant for a job in the advertising or printing industries and you would like to use your resume in this way, take care to keep it appropriate. It is better to be understated in your effects than to have a resume that produces a laugh! A comment about special designs and art work on the resume from a personnel director in the advertising field was, "It is so rarely done well. It usually is a turn-off." This is ample warning that getting too fancy with special designs can do more harm than good, unless your job field is art or design and you are an experienced professional. The typefaces you select should add to the overall effect of clarity, directness, and order.

Proofreading

All of the hard work you have done to produce your resume will have been for nothing if the finished product contains typing or spelling errors. Whether you made the mistake, or the typist did, is unimportant. When you send out the resume, the error is yours. In this section of the chapter, some basic rules of capitalization and punctuation are given. We have also included three sample resumes that contain errors. Read them carefully to find and correct the errors as practice for proofreading your own resume.

Rules of Capitalization:

- Capitalize proper nouns such as names of schools, colleges, and universities, names of companies, and brand names of products.

- Capitalize major words in the names and titles of books, tests, and articles in the body of your resume.

- Capitalize words in major section headings of your resume.

- Do not capitalize words just because they seem important.

- When in doubt, consult a manual of style such as *The Chicago Manual of Style,* The University of Chicago Press. Your local librarian can help you locate this and other style manuals.

Rules of Punctuation:

- Use a comma to separate words in a series.

- Use a semicolon to separate a series of phrases that already include commas within the phrases.

- Use a semicolon to separate independent clauses that are not joined by a conjunction.

- Use a period to end a sentence.

- Use a colon to show that the examples or details that follow will expand or amplify the preceding phrase.

- Avoid the use of dashes.

- Avoid the use of brackets.

- If you use any punctuation in an unusual way in your resume, be consistent in its use.

- Whenever you are uncertain, consult a style manual.

EXAMPLE: PROOFREADING RESUME NO. 1

EUGENE HARRIS

2900 Greynolds Street   Deltona, Florida 32725
Home (813) 555-4625   Office (305) 555-4508

CONTROLLER

Results-oriented financial manager. Proficient in financial analysis,
standard costs, job order costs, budgeting, inventory/cost controls, and
MIS conversions. Experienced with pension programs, insurance,
credit and collection sand bank relations.

ACHEIVEMENTS

- Developed and installed financial structure and controls of a new company which facilitated the sale of the business at a substantial profit within six years.
- Directed the design and installation of a computerized financial reporting system for a growth company without no increase in personnel.
- Supervised the design and installation of a tied-in standard cost system which identified scrap and labor variances, thereby saving $200,000.00.
- Strengthened ivnentory controls, which resulted in a $260,000.00 decrease in inventory and minimal inventory adjustments.
- Decreased accounting staff 20% by converting manual posting to computerized job order system.
- Originated a "sound alarm bulletin which tracked percentage-of-completion of jobs, thereby controlling costs.
- Reduced auditing fees 15% by initiating a procedure for preparation of supportion schedules for year-end working papers
- Initiated and installed financial procedures for a highly profitable turnaround situation.

AFFILIATIONS

Amalgamated Systems Inc.	Finance Director
Charles T. Murrow, Inc.	Controller
The Morris Company	Controller/Treasurer
Adams Cable, Inc.	Controller
CPA firms	Staff Acountant

EDUCATION

Baruch College of City University	BBA Accounting
Pace Univ.	Computer Studies

Proofreading Resume No. 1

The following is a list of errors in the resume of Eugene Harris:

1. There are no dates given for any jobs.

2. The words *collections and* are mistyped in the first paragraph.

3. *Achievements* is misspelled.

4. The double negative *without no* should be *with no* or *without any*. This kind of error occurs as the writer changes her or his mind as to how to express a thought, but does not change the typing.

5. *Inventory* is misspelled.

6. The closing quotation marks are missing after *alarm*.

7. The writer meant to write *supporting,* not *supportion*.

8. The period at the end of the sentence is missing.

9. A *c* is missing in *accountant*.

10. *University* is unnecessarily abbreviated. This is inconsistent with the other use of the word.

Now try your hand, and eyes, at proofreading the second resume. Remember, it may have more than simple typographical errors. Circle each error that you find, and check your proofreading against the list provided after the resume. If you find omissions, write in what you think is missing.

EXAMPLE: PROOFREADING RESUME NO. 2

BONNIE THORNTON

236 Bainbridge Street
Malden, Mass. 02148

EXPERIENCE:

Samuel Gompers Co. CPAs	November 1995
(Boston, Mass.)	to Present

Responsible for the palnning and execution of certified and interim audits of diversified client companies. Duties include preparation of time budgets and audit programs review and evaluation of internal accounting controls preparation and analysis of financial statements, and supervised and evaluation of a number of professionals assigned to each audit.

Other responsibilities include the preparation and Review of corporate and partnership income tax returns.

Industries audited include manufacturing, importing, and real estate.

Lewis, Murrow & Company, CPAs	June 1986 to
(Boston, Mass.)	November 1995

Initially with this firm as Semi-Senior Accountant, advancing to senoirity in 1990. Participates in audits of initially smaller client companies and ultimately advanced to auditing responsibilities with larger accounts.

S.J. Tilden & Company, CPAs	February 1983
(Boston, Mass.)	to June 1986

Gaining my initial experience in the field of pulbic accounting with this frim.

EDUCATION:

Boston College—Graduated in February, with the degree of Bachelor of Science in Accounting. Earned CPA Certificate in August, 1985.

Affiliations:

American Institute of Certified Public Accountants
N.Y. State Society of Certified Public Accountants

Proofreading Resume 2

These are the errors you should have found in the resume of Bonnie Thornton.

1. There is no telephone number by which to reach the applicant.

2. *Planning* is misspelled.

3. Commas are missing in the sentence *Duties include . . . audit.*

4. The word *supervised* should be *supervision* to conform to the rest of the sentence.

5. The word *review* should not be capitalized.

6. *Seniority* is misspelled.

7. *Participates* should be in the past tense, *Participated.*

8. *Gaining* should also be in the past tense, *Gained.*

9. *Public* and *firm* are misspelled.

10. *Affiliations* should be in all capitals to match the other headings.

Now you are ready for your final test. Proofread Resume 3 carefully. Try to find all twelve errors before referring to the list on page 94.

EXAMPLE: PROOFREADING RESUME NO. 3

MARTHA STANTON

PROFESSIONAL OBJECT

To join small to medium sized public accounting firm with a near term goal of partnership admission.

WORK EXPERIENCE

A.J. Jackson, CPA, Lincoln, Nebraska. <u>Senior Accountant.</u> Responsible for various audit engagements, some of which follow: real estate construction-management-rentals, retail-wholesale sales.

August 1998 to present

- Prepared financial statements with all required generally accepted accounting principle (GAAP) disclosures
- Prepare corporation and partnership taxreturns
- Consul ted in accordance with management adsivouy standards

February 1996 to August 1998

E.D. Hills & Co., P.A., Lincoln, Nebraska. Senior Accountant. Responsible for various audit engagements, some of which follows: real estate construction-management-rentals retail-wholesale sales personal services limousine services, restaurants, and employment agencies.

And assisted managers in other various audit engagements, some of which follow: cable television, construction-management-consulting, retail-wholesale auto parts sales, pension-welfare funds.

- Prepared financial statements with all required GAAP disclosures
- Prepared corporation-partnership-individual tax returns including pension plan, payroll, and miscellaneous tax returns
- Consulting in accordance with management advisory standards

January 1994 to January 1996

LaGuardia & Co. CPAs, Lincoln, Nebraska. <u>Junior Accountant</u>. Assisted in various audit engagements, some of which follow: manufacturing-sales of yogurt, real estate management-rentals, retail-wholesale sales, personal services.

EDUCATION

September 1996

University of Nebraska, Lincoln, Nebraska—B.S. in Accounting Activities included: Accounting and Business Club President, Student-Faculty Academic Standing Committee Board Member, Interdormitory Council Board Member, Dormitory Treasurer, and Social Chairman.

MINIMUM SALARY

$75,000

REFERENCES

Furnished upon request

Proofreading Resume 3

The following are the errors you should have found in Martha Stanton's resume:

1. No address or telephone number is given.

2. Part of the word *objective* is missing.

3. The end of the verb *prepared* is missing. This creates a lack of parallel structure.

4. The words *tax returns* are run together.

5. The word *consulted* is spaced incorrectly.

6. The word *advisory* is misspelled.

7. The job title for the second job is not underlined although the others are.

8. Commas are missing in a series. It should read . . . *rentals, retail-wholesale sales, personal services, limousine services.*

9. The layout of the first two job descriptions is inconsistent and peculiar.

10. One of the paragraphs of the second job description begins with a meaningless *and*.

11. Look at the date of the first job and the date of graduation. There is a discrepancy.

12. Salary should not be listed in the resume.

A Final Suggestion on Proofreading

Proofreading requires a complex combination of skills. Not only do you need to know the rules of punctuation, you need to be able to see small errors in details. If you missed many of the errors in the last practice, it is strongly suggested that you have your resume proofread by one or more other people before you reproduce or mail out the final copy. The one person probably least able to proofread the resume is the typist, whether that is you, a devoted friend, or a professional. It is most difficult to see errors after you have typed a piece of work.

If you have now proofread your resume, the last task is—to proofread it once again. Be sure your resume represents the best piece of work you can do.

Techno-Tips

All of the cautions regarding spelling, punctuation, and other errors apply to your resume production whether you are preparing your resume for print or electronic submission. In fact, putting your resume in a resume listing service or otherwise posting on the Internet only increases the number of readers who can see your blunders.

Technology can help you avoid some errors. It is important that you use the spell and grammar checker of your word processing software, but that is not sufficient. Your word processing software will not help you see that you have used a word that exists in English but is not the one you want. It will not pick up inconsistencies in dates or lack of parallel structure in headings. Use the software features but do not rely upon them.

There is one other kind of error that can be created when you submit your resume for scanning and listing within an organization or listing on the Internet. The organization or service can fail to post your resume or post it under the wrong heading. Be sure to check with the organization if you have sent your resume to a company's internal list, and check for yourself where your resume is on the Internet resume list. A check of resumes that I did recently showed an engineer in a listing of teachers. He is not likely to get a call for a job.

In addition, you can create errors when you want to update your resume on the Internet. Be sure you have eliminated an older version in whatever fashion the resume listing service requires. A glance at the resumes on one listing service showed me two by the same individual. In one, this individual wanted a job only in the United States. In the other, she wanted a job only in Belgium. That individual is not likely to be called by an employer. Again, the same cautions on care that apply to printed resumes apply to resumes in all forms. Employers are simply turned off by what appears to be carelessness.

Summary Worksheet

> *There is no one style or paper that is preferable. What is important is neatness, order, and clarity.*

The purpose of this chapter has been to help you present your resume in the most attractive manner.

Use the list below to check on the appearance of your resume.

_____ The printed resume is centered on the page, with at least one inch margin all around.

_____ There is adequate space between lines and between sections.

_____ Each section is separated from the section before it with a heading such as "Education" or "Work Experience."

_____ Formats of headings are consistent.

_____ All dates are correct.

_____ All names are spelled correctly.

_____ There are no typographical errors.

_____ The reproduced copy is clean.

_____ The reproduced copy is on good bond paper, and not onion skin.

_____ I like the way my resume looks.

_____ I have checked all forms of my resume.

Made to order

In this chapter, you will see how to tailor your resume to fit special situations. Four types of special needs are addressed. If you are *looking for your first job,* the first section of this chapter will be helpful. If you are *entering or reentering the workforce* after having been away for a time, the second section is designed for you. If you are *trying to change job fields,* take a look at the third section. If you are *looking for work as a consultant,* the fourth section is for you. If you have some special needs which you feel cannot be met by using the standard resume formats suggested in the earlier chapters, the principles presented in all three sections of this chapter will prove helpful.

The New Worker

One strong common thread ran through the recommendations that employers had for people who are applying for their first jobs—keep the resume concise, keep it simple, keep it factual, keep it brief. Personnel directors and others who do the hiring like to see that the applicant has put serious, effective effort into preparing the resume, and a brief, well-written resume takes time to prepare.

At this point, you may very well be thinking, "But, what should I include?" The following items are the most important, and should be considered first. Then, if you have space, you can add other items.

Education. Use the same information and format as suggested for the traditional resume. Don't try to take up room on your paper by spreading out the items. It should not take four lines to list the diploma or degree you earned, the name of your school, and the dates that you attended.

Relevant and Extraordinary Coursework, Papers, or Projects. Notice the two key words *relevant* and *extraordinary*. Remember most of the other people who work in the field you hope to enter have had the same basic training or education as you. It is expected that you will have taken the traditional courses for the field. Try to look with some perspective on what you did. Ask yourself, ignoring how hard you may have worked, whether what you did was truly out of the ordinary for someone in your field of study and whether what you did relates to the field that you hope to enter.

Extracurricular Activities. There are two main reasons to include these. The first is *to show the breadth and depth of your interest*. List only those activities in which you actively participated. Remember, the person interviewing you may have an interest in the activity you list. The second reason to include these is to *show energy and leadership*. It is important therefore to show any offices you held and your accomplishments within the organization. Remember, however, to keep it brief. The cruel hard fact of the work world is that extracurricular activities are still not considered work. At best, they merely indicate additional skills, interests, and qualities that *might* affect work performance later on.

Work Experience. It is likely that you have had some work experience that is completely unrelated to the job you are seeking. Perhaps you worked as a waiter, a library clerk, a dishwasher, or a camp counselor. Include these to show that you have been serious about earning a living. Do not try to write the experience so that it looks like more than it was. Remember, most people had the same kinds of jobs when they were starting out. The person who will interview you for the job knows that being a cashier in a cafeteria is only very remotely related to a teaching career, or accounting, engineering, or computer programming. Just list the job, with a simple one-line explanation if that is necessary. If you supported yourself through school, that is an accomplishment to note.

Honors. Be sure to note any scholarships you won, distinctions you were awarded for academic excellence, and memberships in honorary organizations. If you made the Dean's List, give dates. If you had excellent grades throughout school in your major, or in your last two years, this may be noted in the beginning where you list your degree.

All of the information tips discussed above relate to the information you recorded in your Building Blocks. Turn back to Chapter 1 and look over that information. Review the general suggestions in Chapter 2 on the use of action words, in Chapter 3 on assembling your resume, and in Chapter 4 on layout and preparation. Finally, use the sample resumes given in the following pages to help you prepare a winning resume.

EXAMPLE: BEGINNING WORKER'S RESUME NO. 1

JUAN C. GARCIA
2103 AFTON STREET
TEMPLE HILL, MARYLAND 20748
HOME (301) 555-2419

EDUCATION:	Columbia University, New York, New York Majors: Politics, Philosophy Degree expected: Bachelor of Arts, 1999 Grade point average: 3.5 Columbia University Scholarship recipient
EXPERIENCE: 7/99–9/99	Graduate Business Library, Columbia University, New York General library duties, entered new students and books onto computer files, gave out microfiche, and reserved materials.
9/98–5/99	German Department, Columbia University, New York Performed general office duties. Provided extensive information assistance by phone and in person. Collated and proofread. Helped professors gather class material.
6/98–9/98	Loan Collections Department, Columbia University, New York Initiated new filing system in this office. Checked arrears in Bursars Department during registration period.
9/97–6/98	School of Continuing Education, Columbia University, New York. Involved in heavy public contact as well as general clerical duties.
SPECIAL ABILITIES:	Fluency in Spanish, studying German. Can program in Visual BASIC. Excellent research abilities.
INTERESTS:	Reading, classical music, and foreign travel.
REFERENCES:	Available on request.

EXAMPLE: BEGINNING WORKER'S RESUME NO. 2

CAROL A. BADEN

Permanent Address:
South East Hollow Road
Berlin, NY 10951
(518) 555-5067

Temporary Address:
150 Fort Washington Avenue
New York, NY 10032
(212) 555-2498

EDUCATION:
Bachelor of Science, Accounting
New York University, New York, N.Y.
Date of Graduation—May 1999 Accounting G.P.A. 3.45
Academic G.P.A. 3.07

PROFESSIONAL
EXPERIENCE:
V.I.T.A. (Volunteer Income Tax Assistance), Spring 1998
Provided income tax assistance to lower income and
elderly taxpayers who were unable to prepare returns or
pay for professional assistance.

Tutor, Self-employed, September 1995–Present
Helped students to better understand the basic concepts
and ideas of accounting.

JOB EXPERIENCE:
Cook, Summer 1995
Prepared and cooked assorted seafood dishes. I was
accountable for deliveries and receiving. (Financed 20%
of education.)

General Laborer and Driver, Summers 1993–95
Operated heavy machinery and was involved in other
aspects such as delivering materials to and from various
job sites. (Financed 50% of education.)

ACTIVITIES AND
HONORS:
Beta Alpha Psi (Honor Accounting Fraternity), Member
Dean's List Fall 1997 and Spring 1998
A.I.S.E.C.—Association for International Business

SKILLS:
Visual BASIC, ODPC and SQL databases, MS Access

EXAMPLE: BEGINNING WORKER'S RESUME NO. 3

Ruth M. David
572 First Street
Brooklyn, NY 11215
(212) 555-4328

Education:

New York Law School, New York, New York
J.D. Candidate, May 1999
    Class Rank: Top Twenty-five Percent
    Student Bar Association Senator, Budget Commission
    Member
    Associate Editor, Human Rights Journal

University of Wisconsin, Madison, Wisconsin
B.A. in Political Science, May 1996
    Dean's List
    Marching Band Drill Instructor, Section Leader
    Residence Hall Council President

Legal Experience:

January 1998
to
May 1998

Legal Intern
Legal Services, Inc., New York, NY

Coordinated rehabilitation services provided to mentally handicapped clients at the Mansfield Training School in accordance with federal and state statutes. Analyzed and documented medical and behavioral data of clients in order to revise clients' individual program plans. Monitored institutional procedures to ensure statutory compliance, and assisted in research for class action litigation. Utilized Lexis-Nexis.

Other Experience:

Summer 1997

Field Manager
Citizen Action Group, New York, NY

Promoted citizen awareness of state legislative process and issues of toxic waste, utility control, and consumer legislation. Demonstrated effective fund-raising and communication methods to the canvass employees. Responsible for developing and sustaining employee motivation and productivity.

August 1996
to
May 1997

Resident Assistant
University of Wisconsin, Office of Residential Life

Administered all aspects of student affairs in university residence halls, including program planning, discipline, and individual/group counseling. Directed achievement of student goals through guidance of the residence hall council. Developed and implemented university policies.

August 1995
to
November 1996

Staff Training Lecturer
University of Wisconsin

Conducted workshops for residence hall staff on counseling and effective communication.

References: Available upon request.

The Reentering Worker

> Use a functional resume to stress the kinds of experience you have had.

All of the resumes discussed thus far have been in the traditional, *chronological* style. That is, all work experiences are presented in the order in which schools were attended, or jobs were held, with the most recent listed first. This is, in general, the style which personnel officers prefer because it is the style most frequently used and it makes it easy to compare one resume to another. However, this type of presentation may not be the most advantageous to you in presenting your skills and accomplishments. For the reentering worker, the *functional resume* may work best. It draws more attention to your skills, and less to the sequence of your work history.

In the functional resume, your experiences are summed up by the accomplishments you have had and the skills you have demonstrated. If you have been a homemaker for several years, perhaps most of your work outside the home has been for volunteer organizations, community groups, or in a variety of seemingly unrelated areas. In this instance, or in other similar ones, the *functional resume may be the best approach to use.*

To produce a functional resume, you need two types of information. First, you need a strong sense of your own accomplishments and skills. Careful and thorough completion of all the Building Blocks and the Skills Assessment Questionnaire in Chapter 1 is essential. Second, you need a list of the duties and skills required by the job that you hope to get, or the field in which you hope to succeed. You can use the Skills Assessments Questionnaire in Chapter 1 to identify certain jobs. In addition, Appendix C in this book lists the responsibilities, skills, and aptitudes required for more than 100 jobs.

Keeping your Building Block information and the job description in mind, reread the section in Chapter 2 on writing job-related descriptions. Begin to construct your resume, not by job title or date, but by *skill area.* All of the instructions given previously on the sections of the resume, on layout, and on production still apply. However, *the work experience section will look completely different.*

The next sample resume was prepared by a woman who worked for several years as a speech teacher and then stayed home to raise her children. In the time that she was unemployed (that is, not working for money!), she carried out several notable civic and community activities. One of these even took her to Moscow as a representative of the United States in her special area of interest. When she was ready to return to work as a full-time employee, she decided she no longer wanted to teach. After some self-examination, she decided she wanted to enter the computer field. Applying for jobs with her chronological resume got her nowhere. All of her accomplishments were dismissed as "just volunteer work" or "just teaching." The following resume got her a job as a systems analyst trainee with a major corporation. This resume emphasizes the applicant's skills and continuity of interest in a highly specialized language—and this skill related directly to computers and how they are used. As a project director, today she often hires programmers and computer consultants.

EXAMPLE: REENTERING WORKER RESUME

Tracy Brinkman
3416 East 57 Street
Cleveland, Ohio 44104
216-555-1384

Objective

Systems Analyst Trainee

Work Experience

Abstract Language Use

—formulated rules and wrote teaching manual for mathematical Braille.
—solved unusual problems in code use for Braille transcribers in metropolitan area.
　　For the Braille Authority, the Library of Congress, and the National Braille Association.

Administrative

—supervised training and maintenance of Braille skills of 20–30 transcribers.
—represented United States at Braille conference in Moscow.
—initiated, organized, and supervised fabrication of 15-foot tapestry by over 300 people.
　　For the Industrial Home for the Blind, the World Council for the Welfare of the Blind, and Temple Beth Israel, Cleveland.

Teaching

—taught speech to foreign-language-speaking students.
—taught public speaking.
—taught use of Braille to blind children.
　　At Theodore Roosevelt High School, Cleveland.

Education

M.S.—Ohio State University—1984
B.S. *cum laude*—Adelphi College—1982

Changing Career Directions

If you are in the process of changing occupational directions, there are several techniques you can use to customize your resume. In the previous section, some tips were given for a reentering homemaker. That is really a specialized form of career change, and many of the pointers given for that resume will also apply. You will also need to use the detailed information from your Building Blocks and your knowledge of the qualifications for the new job that you are seeking.

There are three different techniques you can use to tailor your resume to a change in career:

1. You can use the usual chronological format, *rewriting the description of your accomplishments in terms of the new job or jobs you are seeking.*

2. You can use the chronological resume, *but omit experience that is not relevant to the new job.*

3. You can use the *functional*, rather than the chronological format.

The chronological format is the most useful to the interviewer, since the information is in the expected order. You can list your educational, job, and other background in chronological order and simply omit references to work history that will not contribute to your new job goal. Or, you can list those items very briefly, so they do not take attention away from your relevant experience.

The following sample paragraphs were prepared by a job applicant who has held a job managing an information system and computer center at an educational headquarters in a large city. The first description was used to seek a higher position in educational administration. The second description was used to seek a job in the computer industry. Notice the way the same duties are described in different vocabulary and how each sample emphasizes different portions of the applicant's background.

EXAMPLE

For a higher job in educational administration:
   Designed and implemented all aspects of New York City's computerized career and college information system including development of innovative materials for students, counselors, administrators; supervision of program implementation in more than 50 schools; establishing liaison with central office and school personnel; training of counselors and teachers in seminars and on-site; development of evaluation.

EXAMPLE

For a job in the computer industry:
   Designed and implemented all aspects of pilot and continuing phases of computerized information system including assessment of needs; assessment of costs and benefits of various software and hardware options; cyclical review of all files; technical assistance and training to sites; preparation of varying levels of user materials; integration of system into multiple sites; decisions regarding software adaptation and additions; evaluation.

Example—Career Direction Change Resume No. 1

The first sample resume was used by an applicant who made the switch from teacher to lawyer. Notice in her resume, all of her experience as a teacher is omitted, which creates a time gap of about twelve years. She said that she did not receive many questions on the gap in her life as presented on the resume. In this case, it did little harm to the effect of the resume, and there was no need to try to explain the abrupt shift in careers.

Example—Career Direction Change Resume No. 2

The next sample resume belongs to a man who used it to move from teaching and counseling to personnel work in a corporation. This is in the *functional resume* style, with a brief chronology of work given later in the resume. In general, it is more important for a man to account for all his work life on a resume, than it is for a woman. It is still the expectation of many people that a woman may not work for an employer for long periods of time while she cares for a home or raises children. A gap in employment is, therefore, often less questioned in a woman's resume than in a man's.

Remember in tailoring your resume, you can and should produce more than one version. If you are looking at a variety of different jobs, resumes should be written for each one. The purpose is to use the vocabulary that the reader will recognize as appropriate to her or his field, and to stress the accomplishments that you have had that most closely relate to that field.

EXAMPLE: CAREER DIRECTION CHANGE RESUME NO. 1

SUSAN GRADY

175 West 68th Street
New York, NY 10023

(work)-(212) 555-5926   (home)-(212) 555-4302

LEGAL EXPERIENCE:
    Leonard, Adams & Haber   9/98–present
    400 Madison Avenue
    New York, NY 10021

Associate. Assist partners in major casualty defense litigation, including medical malpractice and product liability. Independently handle own caseload in all areas of defense and some plaintiff's litigation. Experience in motion practice, examinations before trial, pretrial conferences, malpractice panels, jury trials, and appeals. Substantial client contact, reporting on liability, damages, and reserves. Other areas of practice include corporate, contracts, carriers, property, matrimonial, real estate.

    Green & Block   Summer 1997
    532 Lexington Avenue
    New York, NY 10036

Summer Associate.

    District Attorney, New York County   9/96–6/97
    1 Hogan Pl.
    New York, NY 10013

Clinical associate.

EDUCATION:
    BROOKLYN LAW SCHOOL, J.D., 1998
    Awards: Dean's List, 1996–97, 1997–98 (TOP TEN PERCENT)
               American Jurisprudence Award—Labor Law I
               American Jurisprudence Award—Evidence II
    Honors: Brooklyn Journal of International Law
               Associate Editor, 1997–98
    Publications: *Torture as a Violation of the Law of Nations:*
               Interpreting the Alien Tort Statute,
               7 BROOKLYN J. INT'L. 413 (1997)

    UNIVERSITY OF WISCONSIN, B.A., 1983

    COLUMBIA UNIVERSITY, TEACHERS COLLEGE, M.A., 1990

BAR ADMISSIONS:
    NEW YORK STATE, admitted 2/99
    UNITED STATES DISTRICT COURT, SOUTHERN DISTRICT, NEW YORK
    UNITED STATES DISTRICT COURT, EASTERN DISTRICT, NEW YORK
    FLORIDA, admitted 6/99

EXAMPLE: CAREER DIRECTION CHANGE RESUME NO. 2

Gerald Holsten
1205 Maple Avenue
Elsmere, Delaware 19807
Tel. 302-555-7112

Objective: Management position in personnel training and development.

Administration-Development	Developed intraschool program to improve staff morale and instruction. Created a special program for incoming high school students to facilitate their adjustment to a new environment. Administered a remediation and orientation program for newly admitted students to high school. Developed and supervised the operations of a college counseling office designed to service 2,000 high school students. Planned career and college fair programs for students. School liaison to college admissions and financial aid offices and personnel. Published college and career newsletters.
Counseling-Placement	Counseled unemployed clients in a training program for the purpose of job placement. Provided supportive counseling services to clients while they trained for employment. Vocational, career, college, and financial aid counseling and placement for population seeking postsecondary education and training. Individual and group counseling and large group presentations.
Teaching-Training	Conducted sessions to improve clients' communications and job interviewing skills. Trained professional and volunteer staff in college admissions and financial aid counseling. Supervised student-teachers in their training. Taught and developed curricula in psychology, sociology, and basic learning skills.

Employment History

1991–Present	—Abraham Lincoln H.S.
1997 (Summer employment)	—GE Employment and Training Systems
1985–1990	—Thomas Jefferson H.S.

Education

B.A. (History), 1985—University of Wisconsin
M.S. (Counseling), 1990 and Advanced Certificate (Counseling), 1991—University of Wisconsin

Affiliations

American Counseling Association
American Psychological Association
Association of Teachers of Social Studies

Consulting

A functional resume will often work best to help you in your search for consulting work. That is because you are not expected to present your entire work history, only that which pertains to the work you are seeking.

Often in consulting, you are recommended for a position and even have an interview before your resume is seen. Nevertheless, particularly in a large organization, someone will want your resume sooner or later to "prove" that you have the background necessary to complete the work successfully, as a record of what you discussed, or to share with a colleague or partner in making the decision.

Experienced consultants may have pages and pages of related work to report. Just as with resumes for other purposes, it is important that all the experience be distilled to its essence, and that the essence take no more than two pages. The sample consultant's resume shows how to present a lot of information in under two pages. Notice in the resume as well that some information is provided for the major accomplishments, but the usual requirements of dates and names of organizations may be handled with less detail. Of course, you may be asked to provide references, so all that you present should be verifiable.

EXAMPLE: CONSULTANT'S RESUME

Boris Stanton
4321 Hibiscus Way
Miami, FL 33009
(305) 555-6903

SUMMARY

- Systems professional with over 20 years experience as a Programmer, Systems Analyst, Consultant, Manager, and Group Leader. Considerable background in FORTRAN, COBOL, Visual BASIC on mainframes and PCs in a wide variety of technical and general business applications. Holder of BS in Physics, MS in Math, and MBA in Statistics and Computer Methodology. Experienced, comfortable, and proficient in leading large and small sessions.

MAJOR ACCOMPLISHMENTS

- Chosen by consortium of physicians and dentists to evaluate current PC network systems available for office automation and accounting applications. The hardware investigated included IBM RS 6000, SunSPARC, and Windows NT. The software investigated included Oracle Sybase and MS SQL.

- For First National Bank of Florida project managed computer telephony integration to increase efficiency of bank's call center. Integrated network of PBX/ACDs, VRU, legacy databases, desktop applications. First year savings equal $10.7 million.

- At American Limited designed, implemented, and installed a transaction-based bond trading system based on Oracle's DTP and UNIX based X Windows Desktops.

- Instructor at University of Miami, teaching advanced computer science courses, both on graduate and undergraduate levels. Courses taught include Advanced FORTRAN, Advanced COBOL, Statistical Methods, and Operations Research.

- At College of Insurance, led seminars in Systems Analysis for insurance executives.

EMPLOYMENT HISTORY

1978–Present   Independent consultant involved in providing processing services to a wide variety of clients and Instructor at University of Miami, Department of Statistics and Computer Information Systems.

1973–1978   Programmer for ITT and Computer Usage Company. Programmed in FORTRAN, COBOL, and Assembler on IBM equipment.

EDUCATION

City University of New York, MBA, Computer Methodology, 1985
Yeshiva University, MS, Mathematics, 1977
City College of New York, BS, Physics, 1972

Techno-Tips

Generally speaking, the same technological tools that you used to develop and submit your chronological resume can be used for special-purpose resumes such as the functional resume. You can certainly submit a print version of your functional resume for scanning. And you can create an RTF or ASCII text version for attachment to an e-mail submission.

Review all the tips for doing this that you learned in Chapter 3. Remember to keep the typeface and layout simple. Remember to use both nouns and verbs. And remember to use the language and jargon of the field in which you want to work.

It is probably somewhat more difficult to use a structured resume format provided by an outside service to submit a functional resume. That is because the form has been developed to serve the greatest number of cases. And most people do not switch occupations as often as they switch jobs. Although with the fast-paced changes in the world of work, this is no longer as true as it used to be. The best advice I can give you, if your field is heavily represented in on-line job offers, is to utilize all the tools to your best advantage and to think of creative ways that the technology can be of use to you.

Summary Worksheet

> *Keep the resume concise, simple, factual, and brief.*

The purpose of this chapter was to help you design your resume for special situations. To do this, you need to do the work recommended in the first three chapters, and then rearrange and rewrite your resume to fit the situation. Then you must return to Chapter 4 to be sure your resume looks good.

Use this checklist to review the steps you followed.

_____ I reviewed my skills and accomplishments in Chapter 1, "Building Blocks."

_____ I rewrote my experiences and activities using action words and job descriptions.

_____ I read about the essential and optional parts of a resume in Chapter 3.

_____ I reviewed the descriptions of jobs that interest me in Appendix C.

_____ I selected my skills, accomplishments, experiences, and activities that are most closely related to the job I am seeking.

_____ I arranged my experiences in a way the reader can understand.

_____ I looked at the sample resumes for ideas.

_____ I rearranged and rewrote my resume.

_____ I printed and proofread my resume.

_____ I considered how to submit my resume using all available technologies.

Cover letters and recordkeeping 6

> *Use the cover letter as an effective introduction to your resume.*

To handle the distribution of your resume effectively you will need to prepare a cover letter and set up a system of keeping records of resumes you have sent out.

There are generally two ways of distributing your resume. One is to deliver it in person. Perhaps you have an appointment with a contact who you hope will recommend you for a job. Maybe you are going to see a person to whom you've been recommended. In any of these kinds of situations, you will want to have a copy of your resume ready to leave with the person.

The more frequently used method of distributing your resume is to mail it with a letter in response to an advertisement or some other job lead. Whenever you mail your resume, you must also send a cover letter. This chapter will help you write winning cover letters. Appendices A and B provide information on how to find select people to whom you'll send your resume and cover letter.

Remember that the cover letter is designed to introduce the resume and interest your potential employer in reading it, just as the resume is designed to interest that person in meeting you. The cover letter must be neat and clean both in content and production.

Sections of the Cover Letter

The cover letter should include the following sections:

1. Your address (unless it is printed on your personal letterhead that already includes this information).

2. The date.

3. The address of the person and company to whom you are sending the resume. If you are addressing a post office box number in an advertisement, include the box number information. Use the salutation, "To Whom It May Concern:" to open the letter.

4. The first paragraph should explain why you are writing. Is the letter in response to an advertisement, the result of a previous meeting, at the suggestion of a common acquaintance?

5. The next one or more paragraphs should relate one or two highlights of your experience to the job's needs. Do not be afraid to expand this section.

6. The final paragraph should close with a request for an interview and any pertinent information needed to schedule it. This might include hours at which you can be reached at a particular telephone number, or days when you will be in the area if the job is not near your home location.

7. Whether the letter is addressed to a classified ad box number or to an individual, the correct closing is, "Sincerely," or "Yours truly," followed by your signature, followed by your full name typed out.

Writing the Cover Letter

A cover letter, including all the information above, should be one page in length. The language should be businesslike and to the point. Avoid overblown language. One cover letter, after the standard opening paragraph, included the following:

EXAMPLE—PROBLEM COVER LETTER

I believe that my resume bespeaks the qualifications necessary to excel at the position. . . . I have a ceaseless capacity to overcome challenges in skills applications.

The example above is much too flowery and misses the point by hiding it in too many words. On the other hand, you can be too brief. The following letter was handwritten on a piece of lined yellow paper torn from a pad, ripped in half at the bottom.

EXAMPLE—PROBLEM COVER LETTER

Dear Sirs:

Enclosed is my resume in response to your notice in the *NY Times*. My present salary is at $54,000. I can be contacted during business hours with proper discretion. Thank you for your consideration.

Sincerely

Gerald French

Three examples of well-written cover letters appear on subsequent pages. The first two were written to the same company, one in response to an advertisement, the other as part of the applicant's campaign to change jobs, moving to a particular type of company. The third cover letter expands the middle section, speaking directly to the job requirements. This kind of cover letter is very effective when you really know your field. Then you can tie your experience to the job.

Producing the Cover Letter

The cover letter should always be an individually prepared one-page document on good bond paper. Since cover letters must be written to particular individuals, or at least to particular companies, they cannot be reproduced or photocopied like resumes. Of course, once you have written and rewritten your first cover letter to the point where you really like it, you can certainly use the same or similar wording in subsequent letters.

After the cover letter has been printed, be sure to proofread it as carefully as you did the resume. Handle it carefully to avoid a dirty or smudged appearance. Mail the cover letter and resume, unfolded, in an envelope of the appropriate size.

Recordkeeping

In Appendices A and B, you will find lists of detailed resources to help you identify potential recipients of your resumes. Many job hunting manuals emphasize the importance of contacts. While contacts are a valuable resource, many people have found jobs they like through newspaper ads, personnel agencies, and other means. Broadcasting your resume, that is, sending it unsolicited to *many* companies, is not considered by many job placement experts to be an efficient means of job hunting. Yet, there are people who have gotten jobs they really wanted and liked by mailing resumes to all the companies under appropriate headings in the classified telephone directory.

Resume Records

Whatever method of distribution you use, it is important that you keep a record of the resumes you have sent and the results. One method is to make photocopies of your cover letters and to note any responses and interviews on them. Another method is to use a chart like the ones that follow the sample cover letters. A sample is filled in to illustrate how it is used.

EXAMPLE: COVER LETTER NO. 1

THOMAS E. WESTBRIDGE
ATTORNEY AT LAW
5805 GROVE RIDGE STREET
3RD FLOOR
HOUSTON, TEXAS 77061
(713) 555-4322

June 20, 1999

Dept. 12572
1501 Polk Avenue
Houston, Texas 77002

To Whom It May Concern:

I have specialized, for the last fifteen years, in tax planning on the federal, international, and local levels. I am fortunate to have had broad and intensive experience in most phases of the tax law, representing "big board" and multinational corporations, as well as top-level executives. l worked closely and frequently with "big-eight" accounting firms.

I am currently seeking a position with a "Fortune 500" corporation as tax attorney or with similar duties. I would bring to the position analytical expertise as to existing and future tax strategies, acquisitions and dispositions, and compliance.

My primary objective is to secure a position that offers challenge and opportunity to assume responsibility and exercise independent judgment. I believe the enclosed resume substantiates the experience I will bring to a leadership position in your organization.

I am available for a conference with you at your convenience. Please call at (713) 555-4322 during the day.

Sincerely

Thomas E. Westbridge

Thomas E. Westbridge

EXAMPLE: COVER LETTER NO. 2

689 Grant Avenue
Virginia Beach, Virginia 23457
June 21, 1999

Dept.12572
1501 Polk Avenue
Houston, Texas 77002

Dear Sir:

Enclosed is my resume in response to your recent ad in *The Wall Street Journal* for a tax attorney. I am an attorney, admitted to practice in New York. In addition to being an attorney, I am a certified public accountant. I have a master's degree in accounting and an undergraduate degree in finance.

Prior to attending law school I was employed by Peat, Marwick, Mitchell & Co., a large public accounting firm. While in law school and up to the present time I have been employed by a corporation. My current position entails federal tax research and planning, some compliance work, as well as general legal work and special financial projects.

I am interested in continuing to use my legal and financial experience in an environment that will provide the opportunity for continued professional growth. Therefore, I would like to learn more about the position you have open. I would be happy to arrange an interview, at your convenience, to discuss your needs in greater detail. I can be reached during the day at (804) 555-1300, and in the evening at (804) 555-7582.

Very truly yours

Arthur D. DeMille

Arthur D. DeMille

EXAMPLE: COVER LETTER NO. 3

220 W. 28th Street
New York, NY 10011

November 18, 1998

Independence Charter High School
419 East 80th Street
New York, NY 10028

To Whom It May Concern;

I am responding to your need for an assistant principal with extensive experience supervising teachers and staff, administering student services, and planning budgets in public high schools. The enclosed resume outlines my leadership accomplishments in the public schools in which I have worked. I would like to draw your attention to the following achievements which are directly related to a leadership role in a start-up high school.

- In my recent position as assistant principal in a culturally diverse, urban high school, having identified a need, I worked with students, staff, parents, and community volunteers to expand academic and career opportunities and support students so that they would be able to take advantage of these opportunities.

- Immediately before that, I worked at the Chicago Board of Education as a member of the Superintendent's four-person team for redesigning high schools. In this position, I met with community and business leaders and negotiated bureaucratic processes. I also assisted in supervising the Project Directors for the new schools, which eventually replaced poorly performing high schools. While the work of redesign was set within the bureaucracy of the Board of Education, it was one of the early successes in creating smaller, theme-oriented schools that have now taken root in the development of charter schools.

- Before that, as a teacher and counselor in a newly formed public secondary school, in the heart of Chicago, I created a college-oriented counseling program with involvement of the professional staff and support from parents and community. My efforts resulted in students from historically underrepresented populations being accepted at the most competitive colleges and universities throughout the United States. When computer-based college counseling became available, my school was among the first to take advantage of this innovation, and I took the lead.

- In my first high school teaching job, I collaborated with three other teachers to create an alternative education program for students performing below grade level. We drew on resources within and outside the Board of Education, and designed and ran the program utilizing our own leadership abilities and commitment to change on behalf of students.

I look forward to meeting with you to discuss my ideas and interest in the assistant principal's position at Independence High School. I can be reached at 212-555-1234.

Sincerely,

Frederick Bopp

Frederick Bopp

EXAMPLE OF A RESUME RECORD

SENT TO: **Name:** George B. Hayes
                 Title: Vice President
                 Company: Sonotext Systems, Inc.
                 Address: 4044 Garfield Avenue South
                 City, State, Zip: Minneapolis, Minn. 55409
                 Telephone: (612) 555-1096

RESULTS: **Date:** 1/11/99, First Interview; 7/28/99 recalled.
                 Names: Saw Eugene H. Perler; George B. Hayes; Marilyn Mayle. Perler appears to be the decision maker because it is his department. Place of Mayle in decision is unclear.
                 Action: Had two interviews; wrote thank you notes; still seems a possible opening.

RESUME RECORD NO. 1

SENT TO: **Name** _____

                 Title _____

                 Company _____

                 Address _____

                 City, State, Zip _____

                 Telephone _____

RESULTS: **Date** _____

                 Names _____

                 _____

                 Action _____

RESUME RECORD NO. 2

SENT TO: Name _____

Title _____

Company _____

Address _____

City, State, Zip _____

Telephone _____

RESULTS: Date _____

Names _____

_____

Action _____

RESUME RECORD NO. 3

SENT TO: Name _____

Title _____

Company _____

Address _____

City, State, Zip _____

Telephone _____

RESULTS: Date _____

Names _____

_____

Action _____

RESUME RECORD NO. 4

SENT TO: **Name** _____

              Title _____

              Company _____

              Address _____

              City, State, Zip _____

              Telephone _____

RESULTS: **Date** _____

              Names _____

              _____

              Action _____

Use as many charts as needed. They can be made up on 5″ x 7″ index cards and filed alphabetically by the name of the addressee or the name of the company. Check your records daily, and keep them up-to-date. If you do not hear from an individual or a company in a reasonable length of time, you can call and ask if the letter and resume have been received. If not, you can send another one. If they have been received, find out when you can expect a response, if any additional information would be useful, and if there is a set date by which they expect to fill the job.

Techno-Tips

There are two ways in which computer technology can be helpful to you in the distribution of your resume. The Internet can help you target the particular people who should receive your resume. And your own computer can be used to establish your tracking system.

If you have seen an ad for a job, a listing of a job on the Internet, or learned in any way of an organization for which you would like to work, you may be able to reach the right person in the organization by clever use of the Internet.

Here is how to do it. Most companies, not-for-profit agencies, and government organizations have home pages on the World Wide Web. You can often find the page simply by taking a chance on the address. For example, if you are considering applying for a job with the famous White Widget Group, you can type "http://www.whitewidget.com" and see if the company's home page comes up. If it doesn't, you can often find the address or URL on any product or advertising of the company. If that doesn't work, you can try searching for the name of the company using any of the search engines mentioned earlier—www.yahoo.com or www.dogpile.com or others. You can even call the company's headquarters and just ask for their Web address. Once you have found the web site, look for a link to company or organization news. This may include articles written about the company and published in newspapers, magazines, trade journals, and the like. Now use the "find" command in the Edit menu of your Internet browser. Look for words like *said, commented, noted.* You will find the names, and often the titles or positions, of key people in the organization. You may find the person you want to address in your cover letter. Or you may want to telephone that person to learn who the right contact is for your purpose.

Don't be shy. Most organizations want people who have a spark of ingenuity, who can take control of their own lives. The worst that will happen is that you will have no more information than you had when you started the search.

Be sure to include a cover letter whether you are mailing your resume, sending it by fax, or attaching it to an e-mail. Even some of the resume listing databases provide for a cover letter. The more powerful your cover letter is the greater the chance you have learned how to write a winning resume.

Of course, by now, it is obvious to you that you can use your computer to keep track of the resumes you have sent and of the results each step of the way. You can simply set up a word processing file in which you write notes or you can create a database using the fields suggested for the index cards.

Summary Worksheet

The purpose of this chapter was to help you prepare to distribute your resume. To do this, you need to write one or more cover letters. You also need to set up a recordkeeping system so that you know where you've sent your resume, whom you have seen, and which job leads are still possibilities.

Use the checklist below to review your distribution procedures.

_____ I have written at least one sample cover letter.

_____ I have selected a good bond paper on which to print my letters.

_____ For each resume I have sent, I have prepared a separate cover letter.

_____ I proofread every letter before it was mailed.

_____ I have prepared a notebook, index cards, a folder, or a database file in which I keep track of the resumes I have sent or given out.

> *The cover letter is designed to introduce the resume and interest your potential employer in reading it.*

Beauty is in the eye of the beholder

When you write a resume, remember that a winning resume appeals to the reader. This reader, the person who has the power to take you to the next step in your job search, is the reader whose eye you want to catch. Therefore the material in this book is based not only on the author's experience as a career counselor, but on interviews with people responsible for hiring others. The employers, or hiring officials and personnel officers interviewed, were in a variety of industries including accounting, advertising, computers, insurance, law, education, banking, retailing, and health services. They have had responsibility for hiring, at different times in their careers, people at all levels of experience and expertise from beginning workers to the highest level of corporate executives. Although throughout this book they are referred to as personnel or hiring officers, their actual positions in their organizations range from those initially responsible for recruitment to company executives who have the final say on hiring.

The author interviewed these hiring officials, asking each of them a series of carefully planned questions.

The interview had two parts. All of the experts were asked seven general questions about resumes and what they liked, and did not like, to see in them. In addition, they were all asked to comment on the usefulness of specific resume items, such as "job objective" and "age." Their comments on the resume sections have already been presented in Chapter 3, "Assembly." What follows in the rest of this chapter are summaries of their answers to the seven key questions with direct quotations from the experts to help you in designing and presenting your winning resume.

Hiring Officials Answer Questions About Resumes

Question 1

What is the first thing you look for when a resume crosses your desk?

Answers

The most frequently given reply related directly to *relevant work experience.* Some of the items that were mentioned several times were the following:

"Direct experience for the position I am trying to fill."

"A cover letter showing the purpose of the resume."

"I take a fast glance at a person's education. Then I look for specific experiences, ability, knowledge, skills."

"I look for evidence of initiative, intelligence, and energy running through the resume."

"I want a short covering letter. I want the resume on time. If I ask for salary requirement, I want to see it. Otherwise I may be wasting my time, or theirs."

"People in my company need experience on word processors. If it's not there, they are knocked out."

"If it's an entry-level job, I look for the school they attended and their grade point average. If it's for an experienced worker, I look for the type of firm they were with, the functions they performed, and the number of jobs they have held."

"The job experience, especially in the last five years."

Question 2

Many people have resumes prepared by resume services, or have them run off in bulk printing. Others print them on ordinary bond paper. What is your preference about how you want the resume to look?

Answers

None of the people interviewed had a preference about whether the resume was individually printed, photocopied, or bulk printed. They did care whether it was clear and clean. Here are some of their responses:

"I want good, clean copy. I want clarity with headings to organize the material."

"I don't care about paper, but typographical errors are terrible. It shows me the person is careless or lackadaisical. It disturbs me that they would allow this to appear. My business requires attention to detail. If they cannot get their resume right, can they do the work?"

"I don't want anything far out. I don't want big paragraphs with the history of the person. I like the ordinary style."

"I don't care about the preparation, but I don't want a form letter sent out to everyone."

"The resume should be one page."

"The quality of the production is what counts. Is it printed straight on the page? Did they use an ugly, dingy, xerox copy? I like a personalized cover letter."

"The production doesn't affect my judgment unless it's really sloppy—done on some crazy copy machine."

"I don't want onion skin paper."

"Anything over two pages is just packaging. Cut it out."

Question 3

Resumes have many sections—education, work history, professional associations, and so on. Which do you prefer to see first?

Answers

All but two of the experts preferred to see *education* first. One of the officers in an accounting firm said that *work history* should be first. However, he also said that he *looks at* education first. A representative of the computer industry said that knowledge of particular machines and languages should come first. Here are some of the specific comments:

"Education shows you a person's formal credentials."

"Although work history is of first importance, education should be at the top in a very brief form."

"The chronology is more orderly with education first. It helps my mind."

"I like to look at the top line to see how far someone has gone in her or his education."

"The way I read resumes is that I put them in a pile. Then I go through the whole pile, just looking at education, and so on. I want to find education in the top third of the first sheet."

Question 4

Some resumes are written in chronological order, others by function. Which of these styles do you prefer?

Answers

All of the personnel officers preferred the chronological style. Their comments were:

"I expect to see a chronological order. It makes it easier to review."

"The typical person who reviews resumes, reviews many. The best chance to catch attention is to *present concisely*. The chronological order is less cluttered."

"Functional? I wondered where they came from. I prefer the chronological with the most recent first. In the other kind you have to look in several places for work experiences."

"Some people like to use flair. I'm not looking for an artistic flair. I want to find things where I know they are going to be."

The functional resume is obviously not a favorite.

Question 5

What recommendations as to resume writing would you make to a young person applying for her or his first job?

Answers

There were two major pieces of advice: the first was to be *as concise as possible,* the second was to be *factual and down-to-earth.* Some specific suggestions were:

"List only real achievements. If you have none, write a sincere cover letter stating your goals and your willingness to work hard."

"Make the resume fit the job. There is no resume that will fit every job."

"I like to see how well one got through college—interests, honors, energy."

"Show me how your experience in college fits with the knowledge we need in the company."

"Be as terse as possible. Give details on only the most recent and significant experiences. Try to arouse interest in the reader, so you can flesh out the details in the interview."

"If I get a resume of more than two pages from a young person, I'm getting fluff."

"Spend a lot of time conveying what it is you want to say so that you can say it as concisely as possible. I like to see evidence that someone has put effort into the communication."

"Let the resume show me your ability to communicate succinctly in writing."

"Be honest. Be factual. Avoid exaggeration at all costs."

Question 6

What is your policy if you discover that an applicant has falsified her or his background on the resume?

Answers

All of the personnel officers agreed that falsification of any significant data would eliminate the candidate. They said that if a person had minor exaggerations—said they had worked for two years when they had only worked for one year and nine months—this would not necessarily eliminate him or her. However, they all also indicated that even these minor lies would make them uncomfortable and if they had other qualified applicants, they would rather not select the person who was less than honest. Some of the responses were:

"I try to ignore minor exaggerations, but you cannot make up jobs or degrees—say you were a manager when you were a clerk."

"Throw it in the garbage."

"Integrity is very important. Even a small lie is a minus on integrity. If I hired that person, I would never feel sure."

Your best bet is to be impeccably honest and accurate in stating your experience and accomplishments.

Question 7

We began by talking about the most important thing you look for in a resume; I'd like to end with what you consider the worst sin, or most unattractive mistake that people frequently make in their resumes. What really turns you off?

Answer

There are *three fatal errors. All* of the people interviewed mentioned *all three.* The first fatal error is *wordiness.* The second fatal error is *sloppiness.* The third fatal error is a *lack of honesty.* Here are the final words of advice on the mistakes that you will want at all costs to avoid:

"Wordiness makes me think a person doesn't have enough experience."

"Using white-out or other obvious techniques to make changes means the person didn't want to go to the effort of preparing a new resume for my job."

"A lack of parallel structure shows me there was a lack of editing effort. Write, 'I organized,' 'I collected,' 'I assisted,' and so on."

"Don't have spelling errors."

"Don't try to create a false sense of drama and glory. The worst sin is when someone just out of college tries to make a big thing out of a part-time job, and writes 'coordinated sanitary operations' when she kept the key to the ladies' room."

"I don't want to see anything that gives me a credibility problem. Above all, don't lie to me."

"I hate something too overblown, too packaged, with seven or eight pages, and arrangements by both chronology and function. It leads me to question the candidate's sense of herself or himself. My resume should demonstrate what I'm about and show I have a focused understanding of what I'm going after. Poor wording, sloppiness, typos, wrong names and titles are terrible in a resume because a resume needs to communicate a standard by which you operate."

Techno-Tips

All of the comments about the characteristics of winning resumes are true for printed, scanned, e-mailed, faxed, and electronically listed resumes. All employers want resumes that are truthful, that show you in your best light, and that are prepared with the reader in mind. All employers reject resumes that are overblown, empty, or sloppily prepared. However, I have two special tips for you from Internet experts.

The first tip appeared in the "From the Editor" column of *Internet World*. The editor, Gus Venditto, was cautioning businesses to include only relevant information on their web sites. What he wrote to businesses is helpful to us in thinking about the business of writing a winning resume. "The Internet is opening up a whole new range of possibilities, but this is still the same planet with the same human race that was here before the Net was invented. An effective message still needs to be coherent." Follow Mr. Venditto's advice, fill your electronic resume with information about your experience, your skills, and your education. Save the ruffles and flourishes for your personal communications.

The second tip—or really set of tips—comes to you from Fran Quittel (known on the Web as Careerbabe), an Internet career consultant to employers. Ms. Quittel points out that the culture of the Web is a shorthand culture. Your Internet resume should be a teaser, an abbreviated version of your whole resume. Her advice: "Think of the twenty most important words in the vocabulary of your job or profession and use them in short phrases, not the complete sentences of letters or printed communication."

Final Summary Worksheet

Now your resume is just about finished. You have written one or several cover letters. You have decided how you want to keep track of distribution.

You want to be sure that all of your hard work will pay off in a winning resume. This final checklist will help you take one hard, last look at your work.

_____ I have included the essentials—my name, address, telephone numbers, fax, and e-mail address.

_____ My education is given completely, but in just a few lines of type.

_____ My work experience gives dates and companies.

_____ I have included other experiences that show my skills, accomplishments, and energy.

_____ I know why I have included each piece of information.

_____ My writing uses action words and job-related vocabulary.

_____ I have avoided grand sounding phrases.

_____ I have not puffed up experiences to be more than they were.

_____ I like the way my resume looks on the page. There are even margins, and spacing helps the reader along.

_____ I have proofread my resume for spelling and typographical errors.

_____ I have made sure my resume is printed and copied on good paper.

_____ I have looked at the photocopies to be sure they are clean.

_____ I have included my address and the company address on each cover letter.

_____ Each cover letter tells the job I am applying for, or why I am sending my resume.

_____ I have proofread my cover letters.

_____ I understand what employers are looking for in a resume.

_____ I know how to adjust my resume for print and electronic media.

_____ I have written a winning resume.

Appendix A

Sources of Job Leads

Following is a list of resources you can use to locate possible job leads and potential recipients of your resume.

Newspaper classified advertisements

Business, Education, Health, and other special sections of newspapers

Personal contacts through friends and relatives

Contacts made through projects in school

Professional and trade journals and newspapers

Professional association conference placement services (Many provide annual books with listings of resumes and job openings.)

College and university placement offices

Professors and teachers (past and present)

Private and state employment service agencies

Federal Job Information Centers

Classified telephone directories (Yellow Pages)

Chamber of Commerce lists

Unions

Internet sites and Internet searches (See a general guide to using the Internet such as Jandt, F. E., and Nemnick, M. B., *Using the Internet and the World Wide Web in Your Job Search.*)

Appendix B

Additional Sources of Information

There are many directories of business, which are available in business and general libraries as well as on the Internet. Some of them are:

Dun and Bradstreet's Million Dollar Directory. New York.

Standard & Poor's Register of Corporations, Directors and Executives. New York.

Standard Directory of Advertisers. Skokie, Illinois.

Thomas Register of American Manufacturers and *Thomas Register Catalog File.* New York.

U.S. Industrial Directory. Denver, Colorado.

American Register of Exporters and Importers. New York.

Directory of Firms Operating in Foreign Countries. New York.

Dun & Bradstreet's Metalworking Directory. New York.

Bottin International: International Business Register. Paris.

Dun & Bradstreet's Principal International Businesses. New York.

Fraser's Canadian Trade Directory. Toronto.

Occupational Outlook Handbook (OOH). Washington, D.C. This is not a directory of firms or businesses, but is an excellent resource for job descriptions to help in your resume writing or career selection. Current information about the numbers of jobs in the fields, sources of information, and related reading are also included. The *OOH* is now also available on the Internet and can be searched by means of key words, an index of job titles, and occupational clusters. Its address on the Web is http://stats.bls.gov/ocohome.htm.

Appendix C

100-plus Job Descriptions

The following job descriptions can help you prepare your resume in several ways. First, you can use the job descriptions after you complete the Skills Assessment on pages 23 to 30 to see descriptions of jobs that match your skills. Second, you can use the descriptions with the Skills Profile to see what jobs are *similar* to jobs you have already held. Third, in writing your work experience sections of your resume, you can review the duties, skills, and aptitudes you have displayed in jobs you have held. Fourth, you can use the language of the job descriptions when you rewrite your experiences for the resume. Finally, if you are in an early stage of career choice, you can use the job descriptions to help you identify jobs you would like to learn more about.

Accountants and Auditors

Responsibilities: Compile and analyze business records. Prepare financial reports needed for effective management. Devise accounting systems and procedures. Appraise assets and investment programs.

Aptitudes and Skills: Ability to concentrate for long periods; organize work; operate business machines; prepare complete and accurate accounting reports. Memory for detail. Knowledge of accounting principles and methods; data processing techniques. Good vocabulary and communication skills. Speed and accuracy with numbers.

Administrators, Educational

Responsibilities: Manage school systems to promote satisfactory business and academic operations for staff and students. Recruit and hire personnel; prepare and manage budgets. Develop policies and programs. Supervise teaching and non-teaching staff.

Aptitudes and Skills: Ability to analyze problems; organize plans and ideas; make decisions; respond to changing needs; deal with people individually and in groups. Strong communication skills. Knowledge of law, budgets, personnel practices, organizational theory, and educational theory.

Administrators, Health Services

Responsibilities: Coordinate hospitals and other health facilities and their staffs to ensure satisfactory patient care. Organize personnel. Hire and supervise staff. Maintain good public relations.

Aptitudes and Skills: Ability to relate to people; prepare financial reports; solve complex problems; organize and direct large-scale activities; plan and implement policies. Knowledge of financial management; purchasing; fund-raising; data processing.

Administrators, Public

Responsibilities: Coordinate and direct public services to meet the needs of the nation, state, or community. Analyze problems; work with special committees and public agencies; recommend solutions to governing bodies.

Aptitudes and Skills: Ability to relate to and communicate with people; solve complex problems through analysis; plan, organize, and implement policies and programs. Knowledge of political systems; financial management; personnel administration; program evaluation; organizational theory.

Agricultural Scientists

Responsibilities: Apply principles of physical and biological sciences to protect, develop, and manage agricultural resources. Develop methods of growing crops with higher yield and improved strains. Study the characteristics and behavior of soils. Solve problems such as erosion and loss of moisture. Develop means of preserving and developing natural resources.

Aptitudes and Skills: Ability to work with words and numbers; make decisions; use appropriate tools, aerial photographs, mapmaking, and laboratory equipment. Knowledge of scientific theories and data; of physical, earth, and biological sciences.

Air Traffic Controllers

Responsibilities: Coordinate the flights of aircraft to prevent accidents and minimize delays in takeoffs and landings. Monitor aircraft; electronic landing and navigational aids; airport lights. Issue clearances; radar vectors; traffic information.

Aptitudes and Skills: Must have good health; vision correctable to 20/20; clear, precise speech. Ability to work under stress; to think abstractly in order to conceptualize the entire air traffic picture; to establish priorities rapidly; to think clearly in emergencies; to have automatic recall; to listen to more than one pilot at one time. Specific knowledge set by the FAA.

Architects

Responsibilities: Design structures and areas to satisfy a client's functional and aesthetic requirements. Draw plans, sketches, specifications. Monitor building construction. Provide information about building costs and materials. Use CAD (computer-aided design software).

Aptitudes and Skills: Ability to organize; to visualize spatial relationships; to communicate ideas graphically, orally, and in writing. Knowledge of planning and designing, drafting, construction methods and materials, business management. Creativity.

Biologists

Responsibilities: Teach and study all aspects of living matter including the origin, identification, and classification of life processes, behavior, diseases, and structure of all life forms. Research such problems as damage and disease caused by insects and animals. Work in laboratories or the field observing animals and plants in their natural habitats.

Aptitudes and Skills: Attention to detail. Very high intellectual and mathematical ability; spatial and form perception. Knowledge of scientific theories; field and laboratory procedures. Very good writing and speaking skills.

Bookkeepers

Responsibilities: Record day-to-day business transactions on computer and various accounting forms. Prepare summary statements; customers' bills; data entry forms. Sometimes do other general office tasks such as telephone answering.

Aptitudes and Skills: Ability to work with numbers; to concentrate on details. Knowledge of business arithmetic and bookkeeping procedures; of data processing; of bookkeeping software; of business machines. Good eye-hand coordination.

Business Executives

Responsibilities: Develop and administer policies to increase profits and make organizations run smoothly. Review and establish goals; coordinate plans; make necessary procedural changes. Direct major programs. Take overall responsibility for all levels of functions within their jurisdictions. Have "bottom-line" responsibility for profits and losses.

Aptitudes and Skills: Ability to communicate with others; to develop long-range goals and objectives; to establish effective communication throughout an organization. Knowledge of problem solving; decision making; personnel administration; organizational theory. Leadership.

Buyers

Responsibilities: Purchase goods for their firms to resell. Talk with people; negotiate contracts.

Aptitudes and Skills: Ability to work with people; work on details; communicate orally and in writing; work with numbers. Knowledge of merchandising; purchasing practices; marketing techniques; pricing methods and discounting; inventory control.

Chemists

Responsibilities: Research and teach the composition, structure, synthesis, and reaction of matter. Experiment with various substances; analyze data; test samples.

Aptitudes and Skills: Ability to work independently with thoroughness, attention to detail, patience, and perseverance. High intellectual, verbal, and mathematical ability. Above average spatial and form perception. Knowledge of scientific theory; laboratory techniques; principles of chemistry.

Chiropractors

Responsibilities: Diagnose and treat spinal-related disorders to aid patients in regaining and maintaining good health. Emphasis is on the function of the nervous system. The primary therapy method is spinal manipulation. Many chiropractors combine this with other holistic approaches to lifestyle changes such as recommendations for eating and exercise.

Aptitudes and Skills: Ability to work independently; make decisions. Good hand and finger dexterity. Knowledge of anatomy; chemistry; physiology; microbiology; chiropractic principles; adjustive techniques; x-ray techniques; diagnosis; physiotherapy; office procedures.

Claims Adjustors and Examiners

Responsibilities: Review and process loss or damage claims made against insurance companies. Gather facts by interview; consult police and hospital records; inspect damaged property; analyze claims; determine extent of the company's liability. Prepare reports.

Aptitudes and Skills: Ability to deal with all kinds of people; to make decisions; to assume responsibility. Knowledge of laws and regulations governing the insurance industry. Above average verbal and numerical skills.

Commercial Artists

Responsibilities: Illustrate ideas through sketches, drawings, and other works. Prepare artwork for newspapers, magazines, advertisements, book illustrations, designs on commodity packages.

Aptitudes and Skills: Ability to visualize ideas on paper; to design; to prepare mechanicals; to estimate time needed to complete a project; to work under pressure to meet deadlines. Knowledge of tools; layout techniques; composition; software. Aesthetic appreciation. Visual creativity. Form perception. Color discrimination.

Computer Operators

Responsibilities: Monitor and control computers to process data according to predetermined instructions. Select and load input and output units with materials such as tapes or printout forms. Observe the machines for stoppage or faulty input.

Aptitudes and Skills: Ability to approach problems meticulously; to follow detailed and organized procedures. Knowledge of computer systems and equipment; of technical language used in operating instructions and computer manuals; typing.

Computer Programmers

Responsibilities: Write computer programs and other coded instructions for computers to perform a desired task. Decide upon the information needed to solve a problem; prepare a flowchart; write complete, step-by-step instructions. Test programs; correct errors. Write documentation.

Aptitudes and Skills: Ability to organize ideas and data; to communicate technical information orally and in writing; to organize time to meet deadlines; to work with little room for error. Knowledge of programming techniques and limitations. Above average numerical ability and clerical perception.

Computer Repairers

Responsibilities: Maintain and repair computers and computer-related equipment. Install equipment. Provide routine service including cleaning and oiling mechanical parts; checking electronic equipment. Determine the cause of breakdowns and replace parts. Answer customers' questions on maintenance.

Aptitudes and Skills: Mechanical, numerical, spatial abilities. Good close vision; normal color perception; normal hearing. Knowledge of electronics; of elementary computer theory, computer math, circuitry theory; of proper use and care of specialized tools and testing equipment; of appropriate technical manuals; of preventive maintenance recordkeeping procedures. Ability to deal with people; to work under pressure. Knowledge of programming helpful.

Construction Superintendents

Responsibilities: Plan and direct building projects to satisfy the contractor's specifications and schedules. Coordinate the activities of skilled workers, supervisors, and subcontractors. Order tools and materials. Inspect projects and prepare reports on materials used, cost, and progress.

Aptitudes and Skills: Ability to interpret instructions in written, oral, diagrammatic, or schedule form; to understand drawings and specifications; to do arithmetic quickly and accurately; to estimate costs. Knowledge of construction materials and practices; building codes; contract specifications.

Counselors

Responsibilities: Work in schools and agencies to help others to understand themselves better and to apply that understanding to living and working more effectively. May administer tests; interpret test scores; work with individuals; conduct group sessions; do staff development.

Aptitudes and Skills: Ability to communicate well; to accept responsibility; to select tests; to interpret test scores; to help others examine their interests, needs, and goals. Knowledge of counseling theory; interview techniques; developmental theory; world of work; human behavior. Patience. Concern for human welfare.

Dental Hygienists

Responsibilities: Work under the general supervision of a dentist; help people develop and maintain good oral health. Clean and polish teeth; note conditions of decay and disease; take and develop x-rays. Teach patients proper dental care. May sterilize instruments; keep records.

Aptitudes and Skills: Knowledge of dental hygiene procedures such as fluoride and x-ray treatment. Ability to prepare clinical and laboratory diagnostic tests for the dentist; to communicate on a one-to-one basis with the patient; to pay precise attention to detail. Good manual and finger dexterity; eye-hand coordination; cleanliness; health.

Dentists

Responsibilities: Diagnose and treat patients' teeth to prevent and correct dental problems. Most dentists are in general practice. Some are specialists such as orthodontist, periodontist, prosthodontist.

Aptitudes and Skills: Knowledge of diagnostic techniques and treatment procedures; the use of dental equipment; scientific principles. Ability to judge space and shape; to work with people; to communicate orally and in writing.

Designers, Clothes

Responsibilities: Design and construct garments using sketches and sample garments. From these, make full-size paper and/or fiberboard patterns.

Aptitudes and Skills: Ability to sketch ideas on paper; to adapt body measurements to a paper pattern; to sew; to draft patterns; to adjust patterns for fit and appearance; to estimate the cost of making a garment. Knowledge of clothing styles; textiles; fabrics; types of sewing machines; color coordination. Creativity. Finger dexterity.

Designers, Floral

Responsibilities: Prepare floral arrangements for a variety of occasions using flowers, greenery, and artificial aids.

Arrangements must be appropriate for the event and meet customer specifications as to color, flower preference, cost.

Aptitudes and Skills: Ability to work standing for long periods; to lift containers of flowers weighing up to 40 pounds; to work with people. Accurate color vision. Manual dexterity. Artistic ability.

Designers, Interior

Responsibilities: Plan interior space to enhance the attractiveness and function of commercial and residential buildings. Consult with clients and architects; select colors, fabrics, floor and wall coverings, light fixtures, cabinetwork, furniture, accessories.

Aptitudes and Skills: Knowledge of colors; textures; principles of design. Ability to work with people; communicate verbally and through sketching. Creativity. Flexibility. Good business judgment.

Dietitians

Responsibilities: Plan nutritious meals to help people maintain or recover good health. Plan menus and diets for therapeutic treatment; plan menus and supervise meals in hospitals, schools, and other institutions; supervise the production of food; manage food personnel; manage food purchases.

Aptitudes and Skills: Ability to plan and supervise; to work with people such as other health care professionals. Knowledge of principles of nutrition and foods; of personnel management; of financial management. Interest in science; in serving people. Appreciation for food.

Dispatchers

Responsibilities: Relay information, requests, and/or written orders; assign personnel and/or vehicles. Maintain radio contact; keep records of requests and services performed; maintain maps showing approximate locations of workers or vehicles; utilize appropriate software.

Aptitudes and Skills: Ability to plan and direct the activities of workers; to speak clearly and distinctly; to react quickly and calmly; to establish priorities rapidly. Good hearing. Good use of fingers and hands.

Drafters

Responsibilities: Use CAD (computer-aided design) software or hand techniques to translate the ideas and rough sketches of engineers and architects into detailed drawings that enable other workers to manufacture products according to designers' specifications.

Aptitudes and Skills: Ability to visualize objects; to work from written and oral instructions; to do precise and detailed work. Knowledge of the principles and practices of drafting; of tools of the trade, including computer software.

Ecologists

Responsibilities: Study and solve problems dealing with wildlife control, air, water, land, pollution, resource protection, waste disposal.

Aptitudes and Skills: Ability to analyze, prepare, and present scientific information; to work with numbers; to organize information. Knowledge of principles, concepts, and methods of environmental control and resource management. Above average intelligence. Curiosity about the interactions in living systems.

Economists

Responsibilities: Study and teach how people use resources such as land, labor, and capital. Analyze the relationship between supply and demand; determine ways in which goods are produced, consumed, and distributed; study problems such as inflation and recession; carry out studies for government to assess economic conditions and the need for changes in economic policy.

Aptitudes and Skills: Knowledge of the principles of economics; of statistics, research methodologies, and data analysis. Ability to perform arithmetic operations quickly and accurately; to work with detail; to communicate ideas orally and in writing. Analytical aptitude. Above average intelligence.

Electricians

Responsibilities: Install wiring and maintain electrical equipment such as generators and lighting systems. Inspect and service electronic control devices.

Aptitudes and Skills: Ability to visualize objects of two or three dimensions and make visual comparisons; to apply mathematics to practical problems; to read blueprints; to use and maintain tools and test equipment. Knowledge of electricity; basic electronics; planning and estimating jobs; ordering supplies. Good eye-hand coordination. Good manual dexterity.

Engineers

Responsibilities: Determine how to combine raw materials to produce goods or build projects such as roads, dams, buildings, and bridges. Plan and oversee construction and research projects; design, inspect, and test equipment, machinery, materials, and products. Aerospace engineers design, construct, and test aircraft and spacecraft. Civil engineers plan and supervise the construction and maintenance of roads, railroads, airports, bridges, harbors, dams, pipelines, power plants, and water and sewage systems. Electrical engineers design and supervise the manufacturing of electrical and electronic equipment, systems, and machinery. Mechanical engineers design tools, engines, and machines that produce, transmit, and use power.

Aptitudes and Skills: Ability to visualize spatial relations of plane and solid objects; to communicate orally and in writing. Knowledge of engineering and design; of mathematics; of physical and social sciences. High math and science aptitude. Above average intelligence.

Financial Managers

Responsibilities: Analyze facts, prepare financial reports and implement company policies to ensure smooth business operations. Work with other company managers to coordinate plans and provide information for policy makers. Manage an organization's finances; manage marketing or research department. Serve as controllers or treasurers.

Aptitudes and Skills: Ability to work with numbers; to work with attention to detail; to negotiate; to analyze and communicate facts; to develop long-range goals and objectives; to plan, direct, and coordinate programs; to develop methods of evaluating a company's growth, productivity, and ability to reach its goals. Knowledge of principles, methods, techniques, and systems of fiscal and business management.

Fish and Wildlife Specialists

Responsibilities: Research and solve problems related to such natural resources as soil, water, plants, and animals.

Manipulate and manage natural resources for the economic, commercial, recreational, and/or aesthetic interest of people. Survey and restore marshes, lakes, and streams; manage wildlife refuges and game areas; enforce conservation regulations; educate others about wildlife conservation; work in artificial propagation of fishes and in water quality assessment and control; monitor the timber industry.

Aptitudes and Skills: Knowledge of the specialty area or areas as mentioned above. Ability to work alone as well as with others; to write technical reports; to speak publicly. Self-discipline. High degree of academic ability for those interested in research. Good health.

Foresters

Responsibilities: Strive to achieve the best use of forest land and resources for economic, ecological, and recreational purpose. Evaluate forest resources; plan and supervise restoration projects; research and develop methods to protect forests from insects and disease; manage wildlife protection and recreation areas.

Aptitudes and Skills: Knowledge of map preparation and reading; mathematical methods used to estimate future growth; research skills; science; technical report writing; basic administration. Ability to analyze problems related to forest resource management, evaluate alternatives, and make recommendations; to work independently. Capacity for details and standards.

Geologists

Responsibilities: Analyze and study the structure, composition, and history of the earth. Take samples; apply scientific principles; draw conclusions; prepare reports; make recommendations to oil companies, mining companies, government agencies, and universities.

Aptitudes and Skills: Ability to perceive forms and spatial relationships; to communicate orally and in writing; to draw conclusions from limited data. Knowledge of the principles of earth science; of the scientific method; of laboratory and/or field techniques. Inquisitive mind. Extremely high intellectual and mathematical ability.

Graphic Artists

Responsibilities: Create artwork to call attention to products, services, or opinions. Produce artwork for publications, billboards, packages in a variety of styles and media. Create original designs and layouts, prepare sketches, and draw finished artwork. Choose colors, paste up layouts, and mark instructions for printers, often using appropriate software packages.

Aptitudes and Skills: Creativity. Ability to visualize two-dimensional representation of objects; to move from abstract ideas to concrete images; to make visual comparisons; to distinguish subtle differences in shapes and colors; to make decisions based on experience.

Health and Safety Inspectors

Responsibilities: Enforce and advise on public health and safety regulations governing work environment, food, drugs, and other consumer goods. Work with laboratory scientists and other health workers to find and prevent the spread of disease and to ensure the purity of water, air, food, and drugs. Visit establishments to investigate sanitary conditions and collect samples. Visit work sites to identify hazards and make sure safety equipment is used. Examine buildings for fire hazards and soundness of construction. Check vehicles for mechanical problems and safety devices. Teach the public about good health and safety practices.

Aptitudes and Skills: Ability to analyze and use facts; to work with little room for error; to interpret and apply federal, state, and local health and safety regulations; to communicate effectively. Knowledge of basic scientific and/or engineering principles and their application to health and safety. Good observation skills.

Hotel/Motel Managers

Responsibilities: Direct the business operations of hotels and motels. Hire personnel; manage purchase of supplies; determine rates and credit policies; direct publicity and advertising efforts. In small firms, perform clerical functions; relieve the desk clerk; relieve the switchboard operator.

Aptitudes and Skills: Ability to work with people and gain their confidence; to communicate verbally and in writing; to perceive clerical detail; to work with numbers. Knowledge of management skills; accounting; purchasing; personnel administration; hotel operations such as front desk, maintenance, housekeeping, food and drink preparation, service.

Instrument Repairers

Responsibilities: Service, inspect, and install delicate instruments and control systems used to measure and regulate machine operations. Repair, adjust, or replace units in instruments and systems that measure time, weight, pressure, and fluid flow and record data.

Aptitudes and Skills: Ability to apply prescribed methods and standards; to work independently; to use tools and electronic testing equipment; to read and sketch blueprints; to diagnose and repair problems. Knowledge of electronics; electricity; hydraulics; pneumatics; shop math; instrumentation theory. Mechanical ability. Good eyesight. Good use of hands and fingers.

Insurance Brokers

Responsibilities: Sell policies to individuals and businesses for protection against future losses. Analyze the client's needs and resources; recommend specific amounts and types of insurance; maintain records; prepare reports; identify prospective customers. Assist in collecting premiums and preparing insurance claims for clients.

Aptitudes and Skills: Knowledge of the fundamentals and procedures of insurance selling; of details of specific policy coverage; of laws pertaining to insurance; of laws pertaining to contracts, liabilities, income and inheritance taxes, health plans. Ability to communicate by telephone, in person, and in writing. Self-motivation. Self-confidence. Tact. Patience. Persistence. Ability to work under the pressure of sales quotas.

Lawyers

Responsibilities: Advise clients of their legal rights and obligations and represent them in courts of law. Negotiate out-of-court settlements; represent clients before government agencies; prepare legal documents such as contracts and wills; act as trustees, guardians, or executors.

Aptitudes and Skills: Ability to work with abstract ideas; to deal with complex and detailed work; to reason and analyze; to relate well with people; to speak and write effectively; to conduct research. Knowledge of the law and court procedures. Intelligence. Diligence.

Legal Assistants

Responsibilities: Assist lawyers. Research and interpret law sources; interview clients for information; prepare legal documents.

Aptitudes and Skills: Ability to work quickly and accurately; to work with a minimum of supervision; to analyze complex and detailed materials; to communicate effectively orally and in writing. Knowledge of legal terminology and procedures; investigation and interview techniques; particular legal specialties such as corporations, contracts, real estate, domestic relations, estates, trusts, and/or probate.

Librarians

Responsibilities: Organize and coordinate the information contained in libraries and facilitate access to information available via computer. Order, catalogue, and classify materials; maintain the library's collection of books, periodicals, and other holdings; prepare reading lists and furnish access to special information as requested.

Aptitudes and Skills: Ability to understand information presented in verbal or tabular manner; to present information and ideas clearly; to plan and carry out programs and procedures; to work well with people of varying abilities and backgrounds. Knowledge of library techniques, systems, and procedures; of the classification and presentation of information in a variety of media. Ability to use computer search engines; familiarity with the Internet and other computer sources.

Loan Officers

Responsibilities: Evaluate applicants' financial backgrounds to determine whether or not they will receive loans. Review reports of credit analysis; weigh all aspects; make decisions for large institutions.

Aptitudes and Skills: Ability to understand and apply procedures; to make numerical calculations with speed and accuracy; to utilize related software. Knowledge of economics. Financial aptitude. Memory for detail.

Market Research Analysts

Responsibilities: Compile industrial or consumer information for use by companies in making decisions on their products and services. Design survey questionnaires, interviews, focus groups, and other techniques to collect data from consumers. Utilize records, trade and other journals, government reports and statistics to gather information. Analyze numerical and verbal data and present written and/or oral reports of conclusions and recommendations.

Aptitudes and Skills: High ability to work well with both words and numbers. Ability to see important detail and patterns in verbal and numerical data. Ability to work well with people. Ability to make decisions based on experience and data.

Mathematicians

Responsibilities: Conduct research and analyze numerical data to provide information to help solve problems in various fields. Organize, analyze, interpret, and present information in numerical form. Develop theories, techniques, and approaches to solving problems in sciences, engineering, and management.

Aptitudes and Skills: Ability to relate and represent abstract ideas by means of symbols; to generalize from the specific; to think abstractly; to present results of statistical analysis both orally and in writing. Knowledge of mathematical and statistical methods and their use in various fields. Numerical, verbal, and analytical ability. Interest in research.

Mechanics, Automobile

Responsibilities: Repair and maintain automotive equipment. Carry out preventive maintenance; diagnose failures; replace and repair broken parts.

Aptitudes and Skills: Ability to use tools and equipment of the trade; to make an accurate diagnosis and cost estimate of repair. Knowledge of automobiles and their electrical and mechanical systems. Good use of hands and fingers.

Mechanics, Heating and Cooling

Responsibilities: Install and repair refrigeration and heating equipment in homes, schools, and commercial buildings.

Aptitudes and Skills: Ability to read blueprints and design specifications; to diagnose problems in equipment and make adjustments. Knowledge of sheet metal work; basic electricity; carpentry; electronics; math; welding; soldering; and all equipment of the trade. Mechanical ability. Good eyesight including color vision.

Military, Enlisted Personnel

Responsibilities: Employed in various occupations. See job title closest to military occupation.

Military Officers

Responsibilities: Hold leadership and supervisory positions in all branches of the armed services. Most officers are general administrators with technical and managerial responsibilities.

Aptitudes and Skills: Ability to perform a variety of duties; to lead; to work with people of varied backgrounds. Knowledge of administration and organizations. Must be ready to perform work under combat situations. Self-discipline. Initiative.

Nurses (Licensed Practical Nurses)

Responsibilities: Assist in caring for patients with medical problems. Administer medication; monitor equipment; change dressings; prepare food trays; feed, bathe, massage, and dress patients; maintain patients' charts; take temperatures and pulse rates.

Aptitudes and Skills: Ability to work with people; to administer medication and treat patients according to the doctor's prescription; to observe, report, and record patients' conditions. Knowledge of the principles of nursing. Good health. Physical strength. Interest in science.

Nurses (Registered Nurses)

Responsibilities: Care for patients and function as a member of the health care team. Provide nursing care for patients; teach health care; instruct other personnel in nursing skills; administer drugs; perform treatments; maintain records.

Aptitudes and Skills: Ability to work with people; to communicate orally and in writing; to prepare and administer treatment and medications; to maintain charts and records accurately. Knowledge of medical terminology; of the principles and practices of nursing. Interest in science.

Office Managers

Responsibilities: Organize and evaluate office production and procedures to maintain an efficient flow of work. Supervise office operations; coordinate work schedules; maintain personnel, financial, and other office records.

Aptitudes and Skills: Ability to communicate effectively both orally and in writing; to supervise; to evaluate the work of others. Knowledge of standard office practices and office equipment. Good clerical perception.

Opticians

Responsibilities: Prepare corrective lenses and eyeglasses according to the prescriptions of ophthalmologists and optometrists. Fit glasses; sell frames; grind, polish, and cut lenses; mount lenses in frames.

Aptitudes and Skills: Ability to meet precise standards; to perceive forms and spatial relationships; to meet the public. Knowledge of optical equipment; of use of tools; of optical materials; of the anatomy of the eye; of normal and abnormal vision and perception; of federal, state, and local laws governing the ophthalmic field.

Optometrists

Responsibilities: Help people protect and improve their vision. Examine the eyes to determine the presence of vision impairments, eye diseases, or other malfunctions; prescribe and adapt lenses or other optical aids; utilize vision training to preserve, restore, and improve vision.

Aptitudes and Skills: Ability to work with people; to work with small objects. Knowledge of optics; chemistry; pathology; pharmacology; neurology; physiology; anatomy; special instruments and techniques used to test vision.

Personnel Officers

Responsibilities: Plan and implement an organization's policies and programs to attract and maintain the best available personnel. Recruit, interview, and hire job applicants; counsel and discipline employees; classify jobs;

prepare wage scales; administer employee benefit and retirement programs; conduct training.

Aptitudes and Skills: Ability to work with people; to communicate both orally and in writing; to keep records; to prepare schedules. Knowledge of interview and evaluation techniques; affirmative action laws; compensation practices.

Pharmacists

Responsibilities: Dispense drugs and medicines prescribed by physicians, dentists, and veterinarians. Prepare, compound, package, and sell medicines; carry out research in the preparation and effects of new medicines.

Aptitudes and Skills: Ability in science; in math; in clerical perception; to deal with the public; to interpret and understand written prescriptions, formulas, and other pharmaceutical information. Knowledge of composition and properties of drugs; of procedures for testing the purity and strength of drugs.

Photographers

Responsibilities: Record visual images on film to graphically illustrate or explain an idea. Plan pictures to meet special needs such as those of advertising, journalism, industry, or science; develop the film; prepare the pictures for presentation.

Aptitudes and Skills: Ability to perceive forms and spatial relationships; to perceive colors. Knowledge of camera operations; lighting; composition; darkroom procedures; special properties of films and papers. Good eyesight. Creativity.

Physicians

Responsibilities: Maintain and improve the health of their patients. Job duties vary by specialty. There are thirty-four major fields of specialization recognized by the American Medical Association. Diagnose medical problems; prescribe treatments; prevent illness by advising patients on self-care related to diet and exercises; assign routine tasks to other members of the health care team.

Aptitudes and Skills: Ability to make decisions in emergencies; to communicate well both orally and in writing; to work with people. Knowledge of the application of basic science and clinical medicine to the human body; of medical terminology; of physical examination procedures; of modern diagnostic procedures and equipment. Above average intelligence required to understand the basic medical sciences. Interest in science. Good judgment. Emotional stability.

Physicists

Responsibilities: Seek to find the laws that govern the properties of matter and energy in the universe. Make observations; take measurements; develop new instruments. Conduct basic research to find the answers to fundamental questions; conduct applied research to find the answers to practical problems; work at theoretical levels to develop mathematical models to explain the laws and forces of nature; teach.

Aptitudes and Skills: Ability to visualize objects from drawings and written words; to see detail; to be thorough; to write technical reports. Knowledge of scientific theory; application of scientific theory; higher math; of laboratory and field techniques; specialty areas such as solid state, nuclear, and astrophysics; cryogenics; biophysics; acoustics; atomic and geophysics. High intellectual, numerical, and verbal ability. Liking for working with facts.

Pilots and Flight Engineers

Responsibilities: Work as part of a team to operate aircraft. Pilots operate the flight controls; communicate with the crew and with land personnel; monitor flight instruments; supervise the crew. Flight engineers make preflight checks; monitor operation of mechanical and electrical systems during flight.

Aptitudes and Skills: Ability to organize and plan; to work under stress; to make quick accurate decisions; to be able to react quickly to different situations. Good emotional and physical health; good hearing; vision not worse than 20/100 correctable to 20/20; excellent eye-hand-foot coordination. Knowledge of instrument reading; weather conditions; algebra; navigation; principles of flight. Leadership.

Production Managers

Responsibilities: Assure the economical and timely production of a firm's products. Analyze data on costs and market conditions; direct activities of subordinate supervisors; interpret statistics on availability of raw materials; supervise maintenance of plant equipment; supervise quality control; keep records of labor, production, material costs, and equipment.

Aptitudes and Skills: Ability to coordinate people, materials, time; to plan, initiate, and carry out ideas and programs. Knowledge of industry; of equipment; of manufacturing processes; of business and financial management. Facility with numbers and recordkeeping.

Psychologists

Responsibilities: Study the behavior of individuals and groups and try to help people achieve satisfactory personal adjustment. Teach; research; specialize in such areas as learning or perception; provide testing, counseling, treatment in clinics, schools, industries. Perform administrative duties.

Aptitudes and Skills: Ability to communicate well with others; to write well to communicate research and/or diagnostic findings. Knowledge of human motivation; of behavior; of diagnostic techniques; of psychotherapeutic techniques; of administration and interpretation of standardized tests; of research procedures. Maturity and emotional stability.

Public Relations Workers

Responsibilities: Aid their clients in building and maintaining favorable public images. Prepare information about their employers for radio, television, newspapers, and other media; write speeches; arrange for speaking engagements; participate in community affairs.

Aptitudes and Skills: Ability to write and speak clearly and simply; to work with people; to persuade; to organize and plan; to gather information. Knowledge of clients (individuals or organizations); of journalism; of business administration; of public speaking; of the news media; of public affairs. Originality.

Purchasing Agents

Responsibilities: Buy merchandise, materials, supplies, and equipment needed for an organization to function. Analyze needs; develop and write specifications; negotiate with salespeople.

Aptitudes and Skills: Ability to work on details; to work with people; to work easily with numbers; to write clear product specifications. Knowledge of purchasing practices; of contract, property, and insurance laws; of sources of supplies; of pricing methods and discounts; of inventory control; of finance; of accounting; of statistics; of use of computer applications to the field. Knowledge of comparative bidding.

Quality Control Inspectors

Responsibilities: Examine products to ensure that set standards are met. Use appropriate measuring instruments; compute mathematics; monitor allowable percentage of defects; recommend changes in production; write final reports.

Aptitudes and Skills: Ability to reason and make judgments; to present information clearly both orally and in writing; to perform numerical operations; to do precise work. Knowledge of the standards to be met in a specific job setting; of appropriate measuring instruments; of laboratory equipment.

Radio and TV Broadcasters

Responsibilities: Provide information and entertainment by talking to audiences over the airwaves. Read news, weather, commercials, sports, station announcements; act; play music; read and log meters (radio only).

Aptitudes and Skills: Ability to meet a tight schedule; to work with people. Knowledge of voice; microphone techniques; studio controls; turntables, tape recorders, CD players, and other technical equipment; grammar, usage, and pronunciation.

Real Estate Appraisers

Responsibilities: Evaluate real estate to determine its value for purchase, tax, investment, or loan purposes. May specialize in residential, agricultural, or income investment properties. Make inspections; write reports.

Aptitudes and Skills: Ability to catch on to things; to check accuracy; to work with words and numbers; to analyze. Knowledge of the real estate market; of real estate law; of appraising techniques.

Real Estate Brokers

Responsibilities: Bring together buyers and owners of property to work out transactions. Supervise real estate salespeople; sell, exchange, rent real estate for clients; show property; draw up leases, deeds, and mortgages.

Aptitudes and Skills: Ability to work with numbers and details; to work with people. Knowledge of sales techniques; financing procedures; business conditions; property values; laws affecting the sale of property; market values; pricing; clients' needs and resources. Persistence. Tact. Patience. Self-motivation.

Receptionists

Responsibilities: Greet callers at business offices to determine the purpose of their visits and instruct them accordingly. Make appointments; supply requested directions; keep records; send bills; receive payments; type; file; answer telephones.

Aptitudes and Skills: Ability to communicate information accurately; to work with others; to retain a pleasant manner. Knowledge of general office procedures; typing; telephone switchboard operation.

Recreation Program Directors

Responsibilities: Supervise paid and volunteer personnel who plan and run recreational programs in public and voluntary agencies, and private firms. Promote and administer such programs as athletics, outdoor recreation, arts and crafts, recreation for the elderly and the handicapped.

Aptitudes and Skills: Ability to relate to and communicate with others; to plan and implement policies and programs; to establish and maintain good working relationships with staff and clients. Knowledge of a variety of recreational activities; of the personal skill needed to conduct them; of methods of planning, equipping, and maintaining recreation facilities; of first aid.

Salespeople

Responsibilities: Provide customers with a general knowledge of products in order to sell the merchandise. Determine the type and quality of merchandise desired; show various items; explain design, quality, and usefulness; prepare sales slips; receive payment or credit authorization. Keep sales records; stock shelves; take inventories; set up displays.

Aptitudes and Skills: Ability to communicate clearly; to deal with the public; to stand for long periods of time; to do arithmetic quickly; to analyze the customer's wants. Knowledge of merchandise; sales techniques; forms used.

Sales and Service Managers

Responsibilities: Direct the distribution of products and services to customers in order to increase business. Direct marketing staffs; coordinate the marketing process; establish sales territories, quotas, and goals; supervise workers in customer service; monitor recordkeeping; maintain inventories; obtain information from customers on service desired.

Aptitudes and Skills: Ability to plan, initiate, and carry out ideas and programs; to supervise staff. Knowledge of product and/or service offered by firm; of sales techniques; of range and scope of services. Leadership. Enthusiasm.

Sales Representatives

Responsibilities: Sell equipment, services, and supplies to wholesale and retail businesses. Travel to customers' businesses; display and demonstrate merchandise; quote prices; prepare sales contracts; solicit business; keep records; participate in collection efforts.

Aptitudes and Skills: Ability to deal effectively with people; to persuade; to work quickly and accurately with numbers; to work under pressure to meet sales quotas; to perceive details; to work without direct supervision. Some jobs require the ability to carry heavy loads; to drive a car. Knowledge of product or services offered for sale; of sales and marketing techniques; of needs of customers; of employer's credit, shipping, and delivery policies. Initiative. Self-motivation. Patience. Tact.

Secretaries

Responsibilities: Perform a variety of clerical tasks and carry out some executive responsibilities in order to keep the office functioning smoothly. Organize office functions; schedule appointments; screen telephone calls; welcome visitors; type; transcribe; file.

Aptitudes and Skills: Ability to type a minimum of 50 words per minute and/or take shorthand; to follow verbal and written instructions; to operate office machinery; to organize office responsibilities; to spell. Knowledge of word processing; of correct punctuation. Clerical perception.

Social Scientists

Responsibilities: Study human behavior and environment to increase understanding and solve practical problems. Analyze the cultures of various peoples; study the theories and organizations of governments; describe and interpret people and events of the past and present; study the behavior and relationship of groups to individuals and societies; deal with the distribution of people, land and water masses, and natural resources. Work for private and public institutions, government agencies, schools and universities by teaching, carrying out research, and planning programs.

Aptitudes and Skills: Knowledge of the principles of sociology, economics, geography, or other areas of specialization; of statistics; of research methodologies; of data analysis. High degree of rationality. Clarity of expression. Intellectual capacity to understand the basic principles and methods.

Social Workers

Responsibilities: Help individuals and groups solve their personal and social problems. Interview clients to identify problems; develop plans to meet their needs; determine eligibility for assistance, funds, services; aid clients in securing services; record case programs.

Aptitudes and Skills: Ability to communicate verbally and in writing; to be persuasive; to work with many different kinds of people; to handle large amounts of paperwork. Knowledge of sociology; of psychology; of economics; of current social policies; of counseling and guidance principles and practices; of community resources; of interviewing techniques; of agency policies. Understanding of individual rights and cultural differences. Emotional maturity.

Speech Pathologists

Responsibilities: Help people with speech or hearing problems by examining the disorder and providing treatment. Use oral and written tests to determine speech and language skills; conduct programs to improve communication skills; provide counseling; teach; direct research.

Aptitudes and Skills: Ability to speak and hear well. Knowledge of the processes and disorders of speech, hearing, and language; of measurement and evaluation of speech production; of research methodology; of clinical treatment; of training techniques used for individuals with communication disorders. Interest and liking for people. Patience. Emotional stability.

Stockbrokers

Responsibilities: Help people select and purchase stocks, bonds, securities, and mutual funds based on their individual needs. Analyze investments; furnish information about market conditions; distribute information about securities and planning to customers.

Aptitudes and Skills: Ability to deal with people; to work independently; to analyze numbers; to speak effectively. Knowledge of state and federal laws pertaining to securities; of economic conditions and trends; of security analysis.

Surveyors

Responsibilities: Measure the earth's surface to determine the shape, contour, location, and dimension of land and land features. Use information in making maps and charts, establishing construction sites, determining land boundaries. If licensed, may supervise other surveyors.

Aptitudes and Skills: Ability to visualize objects in two or three dimensions; to work with precision instruments; to work outdoors; to sketch plans; to keep notes. Knowledge of math and science; of survey instruments and equipment; of survey and land record laws; of legal principles of land boundaries; of how to write property descriptions; of mapmaking. Physical stamina.

Systems Analysts

Responsibilities: Plan data processing systems to solve business, scientific, or engineering problems. Examine organizational needs; examine existing data processing systems; confer with managers; perform special studies to test the efficiency of data processing systems. Choose electronic equipment suitable to specific tasks; prepare instructions for programmers. Some complete the programming responsibilities.

Aptitudes and Skills: Ability to organize ideas and data; to analyze and use facts; to communicate effectively orally and in writing. Knowledge of computer concepts and limitations. Numerical ability. Persistence.

Teachers, Elementary and Secondary

Responsibilities: Develop and plan teaching materials. Provide classroom instruction to students. Elementary teachers normally work with one group of pupils during the day. Secondary teachers usually specialize in a subject area and work with four to five groups of students in a day.

Aptitudes and Skills: Ability to relate well with people; to persuade; to organize materials and ideas. Knowledge of the techniques used in communicating and generating knowledge; of how to guide students in the learning process; of the techniques of testing and evaluation. Knowledge of the subject area. Capacity for understanding students. Creativity. Versatility. Patience. Leadership.

Teachers, Performing Arts

Responsibilities: Educate and train students in the fields of acting, dance, and music. Prepare courses of study to fit the needs and abilities of students; drill students in techniques; conduct rehearsals; direct performances. May instruct classes or individuals.

Aptitudes and Skills: Ability to communicate; to organize materials and ideas; to present materials on an individual or group basis. Proven proficiency as an actor, actress, singer, musician, dancer. Creativity. Versatility. Patience. Leadership.

Teachers, University and College

Responsibilities: Educate and train students. Prepare and present materials; evaluate students through assigned problems, discussions, research papers, laboratory work, and examinations. Engage in research and writing. Serve as advisors to students. Serve as consultants to industry and government.

Aptitudes and Skills: Ability to work with ideas and concepts; to communicate effectively; to relate to a wide variety of students. Knowledge of one's field; of evaluation. Self-discipline. Good judgment.

Technicians, Broadcast

Responsibilities: Install, operate, and maintain electronic equipment used to record or transmit radio and television programs.

Aptitudes and Skills: Ability to visualize objects of two or three dimensions; to work under stress. Knowledge of broadcast equipment; of electronics principles; of test equipment such as oscilloscopes; of the use of related tools such as soldering irons. Facility for math. Good color vision.

Technicians, Dental Lab

Responsibilities: Make and repair dentures, crowns, bridges, and other dental appliances according to dentists' prescriptions. Study the dentist's prescription; plan the sequence of work; design, construct, and repair the dentures.

Aptitudes and Skills: Ability to perceive forms and spatial relationships; to carry out detailed work; to work under pressure to meet deadlines; to use laboratory tools and equipment safely. Knowledge of oral anatomy; dental lab techniques; technical vocabulary; characteristics of materials used. Finger and manual dexterity. Patience. Artistic ability.

Technicians, Electronics

Responsibilities: Help engineers design and develop electronic equipment and electrical machinery. Products include semiconductors, transformers, computers, industrial and medical measuring or control devices. Use information from blueprints and detailed drawings; test, adjust, and inspect products; ensure that set standards and specifications have been met; repair and service defective equipment.

Aptitudes and Skills: Ability to express ideas and information clearly both orally and in writing; to work with numbers; to analyze technical information; to notice and compare differences in objects; to work to detailed specifications; to do precise work. Knowledge of math and related fields of science; technical blueprint reading; drafting; basic electrical engineering procedures.

Technicians, Emergency Medical

Responsibilities: Provide immediate care to the critically ill and injured. May transport patients to hospitals. Determine the nature and extent of illness or injury; provide first aid; lift and carry patients on stretchers; radio the patient's condition to medical personnel at the hospital. Inspect and maintain ambulance and emergency equipment.

Aptitudes and Skills: Ability to work with people who are injured or in a state of shock; to lift and carry patients. Knowledge of life support and emergency treatment procedures; of the care and use of emergency equipment; of the repair and maintenance of ambulances; of sanitizing and disinfecting procedures.

Technicians, Health

Responsibilities: Use sophisticated medical equipment to aid in the diagnosis and therapy of various health problems. Some technicians specialize in the operation of electrocardiograph, electroencephalograph, or dialysis equipment; others specialize in preparing operating room equipment; others specialize in constructing and fitting braces and artificial limbs.

Aptitudes and Skills: Ability to work with equipment; to work with patients; to perceive forms and spatial relationships. Knowledge of medical equipment; medical terminology.

Technicians, Medical Records

Responsibilities: Maintain files of information on patients for hospitals and other health facilities. Analyze and code information; review records for accuracy; compile statistics; prepare reports; supervise clerks.

Aptitudes and Skills: Ability to work accurately; to communicate orally and in writing; to work with data; to work with people. Knowledge of information storage system; evaluation of health records; medical terminology; statistical recording.

Technicians, Nuclear Power

Responsibilities: Operate machines to produce nuclear fuels and to control nuclear reactors. Control equipment to extract uranium and other radioactive materials; use sandblasting machines and chemicals to clean radioactive equipment; control reactors used in scientific tests; observe gauges; adjust controls; load and unload nuclear fuel elements; seal radioactive waste in lead and concrete containers.

Aptitudes and Skills: Ability to carry out instructions with precision; to deal with stress; to work with machines. Knowledge of nuclear processes and techniques; clerical recordkeeping; mechanics; electronics.

Technicians, Radio and TV Service

Responsibilities: Install and repair electrical and electronic equipment such as radios, TVs, CD players, tape recorders, and electronic instruments.

Aptitudes and Skills: Ability to manipulate parts and tools; to follow diagrams and manufacturers' specifications. Knowledge of basic math; of electronics circuitry and components; of appropriate tools and testing devices; of diagnosing problems; of making repairs.

Therapists, Occupational

Responsibilities: Plan and organize activities to help rehabilitate patients who are physically or mentally disabled.

Direct educational, vocational, and recreational activities; evaluate the abilities and skills of patients; set goals for patients; plan therapy programs; work with other members of the medical staff.

Aptitudes and Skills: Ability to work with others; to communicate with patients and staff; to maintain records of patients' progress. Knowledge of therapy programs; equipment and materials used in therapy programs; anatomy; neuroanatomy; kinesiology; activity analysis. Patience. Manual skill. Interest in serving people.

Therapists, Physical

Responsibilities: Treat individuals with physical disabilities to relieve pain and restore function. Plan and administer treatments prescribed by a physician; administer and interpret tests and measurements for muscle strength, coordination, respiratory and circulatory efficiency; develop programs for treatment; instruct patients in the care and use of wheelchairs, braces, crutches, and other devices; keep records of treatment.

Aptitudes and Skills: Ability to work toward long-range goals; to work with people; to communicate with patients and members of the medical team. Knowledge of principles, techniques, materials, and equipment used in physical therapy; of how to adapt treatment to individual patients; of human growth and development; of human anatomy and physiology; of how to repair and/or construct needed equipment; of community resources. Stamina. Patience. Interest in people.

Travel Agents

Responsibilities: Provide travel information and make travel arrangements that meet client's budget, interest, and time. Use timetables, travel manuals, rate books; plan routes; compute costs; verify arrival and departure times and seating space.

Aptitudes and Skills: Ability to work with people; to work with details; to do several things at one time; to work easily on the telephone; to communicate information accurately; to keep up with frequent changes in information.

Underwriters

Responsibilities: Review insurance applications, determine the degree of risk involved, and accept applications following company policy. Look at applications; examine medical reports; review actuarial tables; make judgments; outline the terms of the contract and premium rates. Correspond with policyholders, agents, and managers. Specialize in life, property and liability, or health insurance policies for individuals or groups.

Aptitudes and Skills: Ability to make prompt decisions; to communicate with others; to catch onto things easily; to work with details; to gather and evaluate information; to write reports. Knowledge of company's policies; of the various types of insurance; of methods of rating policies; of statistical interpretation.

Urban and Regional Planners

Responsibilities: Prepare for the overall growth and improvement of urban, suburban, and rural areas. Plan for solutions to problems in areas such as land use, housing, transportation, and environmental resources. Prepare studies that show how land is currently being used; propose ways to develop unused land; suggest improvements to existing facilities to meet future needs. Meet with citizens' groups. Speak before planning committees.

Aptitudes and Skills: Ability to work with people; to communicate orally and in writing; to make evaluations; to work with data; to visualize objects mentally; to perceive detail. Knowledge of governmental organizations and regulations; of the principles of planning; of social and environmental problems.

Veterinarians

Responsibilities: Prevent, control, and cure animal diseases. Diagnose and prescribe treatment for companion animals and herd animals. Carry out regulatory and public health functions; research; teach; supervise veterinary technicians.

Aptitudes and Skills: Ability to work with animals. Knowledge of animal anatomy; physiology; pathology; biochemistry; diagnosis and treatment of animal disease; surgical techniques. Intelligence. Manual dexterity. Interest in science.

Word Processors

Responsibilities: Type and edit documents using current software packages. Receive material to type in either handwritten or typed form or on prerecorded cassettes; format the document; type the text; submit the text for proofreading; use the text editing functions of the software to correct copy.

Aptitudes and Skills: Ability to understand and carry out instructions; to check accuracy; to distinguish between different types of documents; to type a minimum of 50 to 60 words per minute. Knowledge of formats for letters, statistical reports, and other documents; of personal computers as they relate to word processing; of spelling, grammar, and punctuation.

Writers and Editors

Responsibilities: Communicate news and ideas as accurately and clearly as possible to specific audiences. Gather and evaluate facts; write stories or articles; produce technical reports; write advertising copy. Edit material so that it fits the style and space for which it is intended.